the
candle
maker

the
candle
maker

Claire Leavey

NORTH LIGHT BOOKS

Cincinnati, Ohio

For my daughter, Gabriel

First published in Great Britain in 2002 by
Collins & Brown Limited
64 Brewery Road
London N7 9NT

A member of the Chrysalis Group plc

First published in North America
in 2002 by North Light Books
an imprint of F&W Publications
4700 East Galbraith Road
Cincinnati, Ohio 45236

Project managed by **Emma Baxter**
Edited by **Michelle Pickering**
Designed by **Ruth Hope**
Photography by **Siân Irvine**

1 3 5 7 9 8 6 4 2

Reproduction by Classicscan Ltd, Singapore
Printed and bound by C&C Offset, Hong Kong

ISBN 1-58180-250-1

Library of Congress Cataloging-in-Publication Data is available.

Note Detailed safety information
is provided on pp. 16–17. The author,
publisher, and copyright owner accept no responsibility
for any damage or injury caused or sustained while using the
products or techniques outlined in this book.

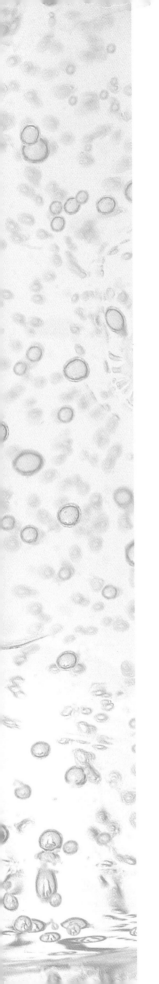

contents

introduction

In this hectic modern world, where every feature of life seems to be driven by a relentless stream of electricity, it is sometimes hard to find a corner you can truly call a sanctuary. However, by harnessing the gentle power of candlelight, you can transform your home into a magical oasis of calm.

For thousands of years, candlelight was the only means of illumination after sundown. Slices of soft wax were rolled together around a wick to create solid, sturdy cylinders, or molten wax was poured along huge lengths of wick to create awe-inspiring ecclesiastical candles. Liquid vegetable oil and a range of animal fats provided cheaper forms of lighting, but despite the smoke and smell of some of these inferior fuels, the glamour of their gentle illumination was the same. It was only in the mid-nineteenth century that paraffin wax came on the scene, and with oil lamps, gas, and electricity hot on its heels, this versatile and easily managed material barely established itself as a practical means of lighting before candles became a derided archaism, or at best an eccentric luxury. However, in our insanely humming modern world, the soporific lure of candlelight is once more proving irresistible.

Bathe by the light of a battery of tapers, and more than just your body will feel refreshed. Relax to music, soothed by the flickering glow of a fragrant pillar candle, and the aromatic oils will lift your spirits until they soar with the song. And it is not just using candles that is great therapy—the meditative rhythms of making them are also infinitely soothing.

From the simplest rolled beeswax sheets to elaborate special-effect finishes, candle making is easy to get into—and utterly seductive once you have started. With basic household equipment plus a couple of specialist essentials, you can begin to create the means of your own liberation. This book explains all the materials and techniques required, and gives complete instructions for making 36 inspirational projects. So work your way through these pages and dispel the shadows from your life.

Candlelight can add glamour to quite ordinary surroundings and create the perfect atmosphere for unwinding. Be inventive about where you place candles in your home, but remember to keep flames well away from curtains and flammable surfaces. If you are placing candles low down, as shown here, make sure they are clearly visible, and placed well away from any edges.

indoor moods

Candles transform any environment into an inspirational, mysterious world, but it is inside your home that their magic will be especially potent. With the help of a few thoughtfully positioned candles, you can transform your everyday living space into a place of enchantment.

The two rooms that most benefit from thoughtful use of candles are the bathroom and sitting room. The sitting room is generally large enough to allow the imagination free rein, and so it is here that you can have the most fun in making a truly magical candle display. However, this room also brings the greatest safety problems, so ensure that you use reliable stands and avoid placing candles unprotected at a height at which they could cause disaster for children, cats or skirts.

In most bathrooms, there is little risk of fire, but here you may struggle to combine practicality with an inspiring display. If the room is tiny, a wall-mounted multiple stand will solve the problem. Another great bathroom idea is to use lots of hinged candle stands from old pianos to make attractive foldaway holders.

Whichever room you wish to decorate with candles, think about the following tricks to achieve your desired look.

candle power

Increase candle power in shadowy corners by ranking candles in groups, or by using multiwick candles in place of conventional

Filling an old fireplace with candles can transform a living room, providing a central focus of warmth and intimacy.

Place candles around your bath and make candlelight an integral part of your relaxation routine.

single-wick versions. Shadowy corners and seating areas can benefit greatly from this.

positioning candles

Placing candles at a low level creates a dramatic effect. Fill a fireplace with candles (behind a mesh guard), or place them on side tables to light your room from beneath. Pay special attention to safety—candles on or near the floor can be overlooked and knocked into. Hurricane lamps are a safe option as they surround the flame, protecting feet and long skirts from danger.

Mounting candles on walls completes any lighting scheme. Use in conjunction with mirrors, or illuminate focal points such as favorite paintings, photographs, or architectural features.

Candles mounted high up shed a little light a long way, and are ideal for intimate dining, where atmosphere and practicality are prime considerations. The classic chandelier combines refractive and reflective crystal drops with candlelight to create a sparkling ambience.

aroma

Aroma is as important to the ambience of a room as decoration. Naturally scented candles produce the most exquisite fragrances—and, if you select them according to aromatherapy principals, will make a change of mood as easy as striking a match. See pp. 44–45 for advice on adding scented inclusions, candle perfume, and essential oils to your candles, as well as instructions for making a vapor lamp.

Use your imagination when designing with candles, the results are always a talking point.

outdoor magic

Nothing matches the drama and intimacy of an illuminated summer garden. By combining a natural setting with the beauty of a living flame you can create a truly enchanted world. Candlelight links the garden to the rest of the house, encouraging guests outside. Let your imagination go wild...

The garden is the place where your dramatic instinct can run riot with candle flame. As long as you pay proper attention to the siting of your candles, there are no special safety considerations to hold you back. Paving, soil,

and water make natural firebreaks, so any mishap will be automatically contained. Just be sure to position candles well away from foliage, and place any small candles used along pathways sufficiently away from human traffic, and at waist height or above, so that people realize they are there.

In planning an outdoor lighting scheme, the most important thing to bear in mind is that the night does not reflect, so the throw of each flame will extend only as far as those objects nearest to the light source. This is why lighting a garden is always a dramatic affair, even if your scheme consists of nothing more than an old oil lamp on a table.

If you have a small urban space, think about using available walls or fences as surfaces to bounce off light. Polished copper panels or ordinary mirrors are ideal for this. In the country, you will have fewer surfaces to reflect the light but a broader canvas against which to arrange your candles. Hang lanterns

An array of tiny lights makes for a beautiful focal point in the garden. Use them to accent favorite areas or a dark corner which needs enlivening.

Wind protection is key to garden lighting—buy purpose-made shades or make your own. Here, container candles have been carefully placed in the centre of large paper bags.

from trees, use huge medieval tapers in the borders, and stand enormous citronella pots on the terraces to repel winged invaders.

If your garden is well protected from the breeze, ordinary sconces can look sensational. Specially designed wind-proof sconces, lanterns, and hurricane lamps are readily available, or you could make your own wind-protectors from old tin cans, piercing them with a hammer and nail for a pretty effect. Bear in mind the following design tips when lighting your garden:

accent

The best way to think of outdoor candles is as highlights for accent points around the garden. Without nearby surfaces to reflect the light, your candles will be wasted, so position them near things you want to emphasize.

light from the ground

Under-lit feature plants or statues can look sensational, and large, sculptural container candles often prove the finishing touch to a paved area. Beware, however, when lighting paths. Rows of tiny tea lights may look lovely, but if the area is going to be crowded, the potential danger makes their use impractical.

hanging overhead

Candles mounted high up in trees or arbors produce an intimate, enclosed feel. Emphasizing the leaves or the roof of a summer house can create the impression of a ceiling—one that disappears with the dawn. Hanging lights can also create the atmosphere of a grotto.

aroma

There is little point in using aromatic candles outside, since their scent will be carried away quickly on the breeze. Citronella, however, is an extremely useful outdoor candle. While you might not be able to smell it, it is a great means of repelling bothersome insects.

stands and fittings

There are as many different sorts of candle stands, sticks, lamps, and fittings as there are candles. Your own taste and decor will be the ultimate deciders in how you choose to display the candles you make, but their shape, size, weight, candle power, and intended setting will all play roles as well.

If you are looking for **antique candlesticks** and candelabra in crystal, silver, or brass, they can be very expensive for a special pair. However, you can often find odd candlesticks at antique sales at a much cheaper price, and a collection of these can make a wonderful feature for a mantel. Old crystal chandeliers—even quite recent, relatively plain ones—are always expensive, so if you are thinking of buying, be prepared to pay quite a lot. Bear in mind also that a valuable

chandelier should always be transported and installed by a specialist company.

Most genuine antique candleholders can be closely matched by modern reproductions, or even outshone by contemporary designs on a similar theme. You can usually tell a genuine antique by one important feature: the candle-holder will actually lift out from the ornate main fitting. They were made like this so servants could collect the holders and clean out the old wax stubs.

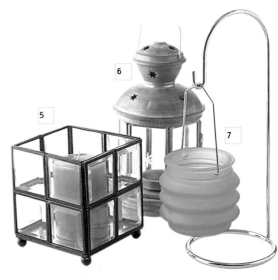

Tea light holders come in an amazing array of different forms: from little glass shades, through aromatherapy lamps, to heavy, masculine slabs of slate with deep recesses stamped into them. If you're thinking of making your own tin-can hurricane lamps for use outdoors, tea lights are the obvious choice to use with them.

A candlestick is just that—an upright stick with either a "pricket" (a spike), or a collar, to hold the candle firmly in place at the top of the stick.

Any branched tabletop or wall-mounted candleholder is a candelabra, and each of its arms is known as a candelabrum.

Sconces are wall-mounted candleholders, sometimes with two or more branches, and always with a reflective backplate of some sort. When mounting your candles be careful to avoid placing them too close to the wall. Otherwise, you are likely to sustain smoke damage once they have been lit.

A candle lamp is a glazed box with a little door and controlled ventilation, used to protect the flame from wind. They are useful for the garden, or to prevent candle smoke from smogging up walls.

Tabletop, blown-glass hurricane lamps originated in the colonial Caribbean. Hanging hurricane lamps, blown through metal collars, are of Indian origin. It is best to choose a fat cylinder candle to stand in the bottom of either of these lamps.

Opposite page: *Modern wrought-iron versions of traditional candleholders, and a selection of lanterns.*
This page: *Container candles have built-in stands, while tea lights are inexpensive and easy to use.*

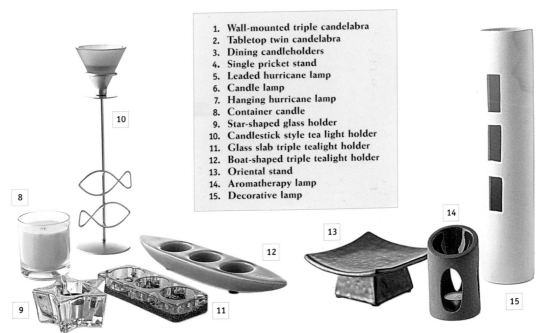

1. Wall-mounted triple candelabra
2. Tabletop twin candelabra
3. Dining candleholders
4. Single pricket stand
5. Leaded hurricane lamp
6. Candle lamp
7. Hanging hurricane lamp
8. Container candle
9. Star-shaped glass holder
10. Candlestick style tea light holder
11. Glass slab triple tealight holder
12. Boat-shaped triple tealight holder
13. Oriental stand
14. Aromatherapy lamp
15. Decorative lamp

getting started

safety

When working with liquid wax, it is important to observe a few basic ground rules, both to ensure your own safety and to guard against damage to textiles and surfaces around your work area.

Molten wax is difficult to remove from textiles, so wear old clothes and shoes with smooth-surfaced uppers. Wear a sturdy apron to protect your clothes from splashes. Avoid wearing anything that might shed fibers, since these could find their way into the wax and ruin your candles. Always use oven mitts when handling hot cans and saucepans.

cleaning spills

When melting wax, leave at least 2" (5cm) of the container unfilled to prevent spills. This is particularly important when dipping because wax could overflow. If you do spill wax, allow any splashes that fall on the floor or work surface to set, then scrape them off with a wooden spatula. If wax splashes onto textiles, place paper towels onto the affected area and iron over them on a low setting. Repeat with fresh paper until all traces of wax have been lifted out.

dealing with scalds

The temperatures at which wax is used in most of the projects in this book would not cause a scald if you splashed any on your skin, though it would certainly hurt for a moment. However, when working with jelly wax or creating high-temperature special effects, you should take extra care to avoid spilling wax on yourself. If you do splash your skin, allow the wax to set, then peel off. If you are worried that the wax is hot enough to burn, plunge the affected area into cold water to accelerate setting and alleviate pain. If you are concerned about getting wax in your eyes,

Dealing with a wax fire It is essential not to allow wax to overheat or it could become highly combustible. To ensure that it does not, always melt wax in a double boiler and check the temperature with a thermometer. As with oils, if the boiling point is reached you will see no telltale bubbles. The first signs of an impending inferno will be a strong smell and smoke rising from the surface of the molten wax. By this stage, you are on the verge of real trouble, so switch off the heat source immediately and allow to cool. If your wax does catch fire, switch off the heat source and deal with the burning wax in the same way as cooking oil. Do not use water to extinguish the flames, but instead smother with a purpose-made fire blanket or kitchen towel soaked in cold water and wrung out. Try to memorize this information before starting work.

you could wear laboratory goggles, though these can make it harder to see what you are doing and as a result can cause accidents.

leftover wax

Always pour leftover wax into flexible plastic or foil containers at the end of a candle-making session. Once set, squeeze the containers to remove the wax, which can then be stored for later use. It is best to choose relatively small containers, because small quantities of wax melt more quickly than large ones. Never try to remelt wax that has set in its melting pot. If you do so, the layer of wax across the top of the vessel will be the last to melt. Meanwhile, the liquid wax beneath will expand and create pressure. The result would be a miniature volcano of liquid hot wax, erupting from the crust with no warning at all.

design considerations

Always consider safety when designing candles. Are the wick dimensions correct? Will the candles stand securely? Are the inclusions flammable? You will no doubt have seen dried or silk flowers, raffia, bark, and other materials used to create delightful arrangements with candles at their heart. By all means be inventive with the materials you choose to decorate candles, but always bear in mind that these items easily catch fire. Even if you are confident that your candle has been safely made, you should never leave it burning unattended, even for a moment.

safety checklist

Always make sure that you have the following items at hand when working with molten wax:

- Apron
- Oven mitts
- Double boiler
- Fire blanket or wet cloth
- Thermometer

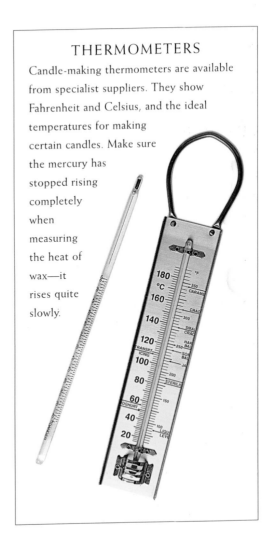

THERMOMETERS

Candle-making thermometers are available from specialist suppliers. They show Fahrenheit and Celsius, and the ideal temperatures for making certain candles. Make sure the mercury has stopped rising completely when measuring the heat of wax—it rises quite slowly.

paraffin wax and beeswax

Do you want the instant gratification of paraffin wax or the natural purity of beeswax? Paraffin wax offers an astounding range of colors and special effects, while beeswax creates sweet-smelling candles that are slow to make and slow to burn.

paraffin wax

Paraffin wax dates from as recently as the mid-1800s, but has all but taken over from beeswax as the candle maker's material of choice. This colorless, odorless by-product of the petrochemical industry is fast-melting, infinitely adaptable, and easy to use. It is a wonderful material with which to start candle making, for it also enjoys fast cooling, which means that you get to see the fruits of your efforts quickly.

Paraffin wax is refined from mineral oil, so just like diamonds it starts life as a black substance that is transformed into a prized, colorless material. Universally available in convenient pellets, the wax pictured here has been melted and tinted with swirls of pink and blue.

Paraffin wax is solid at room temperature, but melts quickly once it is heated to around 140–149°F (60–65°C). A range of different qualities and structures are available, melting at anything from 104–160°F (40–71°C), but the kind of wax most commonly available for candle making lies in the middle temperature range. You can use it on its own, but more usually stearin is added to improve burning, assist molding, and to clarify the wax's structure, giving it a glossy surface.

When molten, paraffin wax is as thin as water, and becomes a sort of limp gelatin as it sets. When the final stages of hardening are reached, the wax suddenly turns from a pliable, rubbery state to a hard, brittle consistency that makes a bright plinking sound when tapped. Paraffin wax takes color superbly, and there is a real rainbow of dyes you can choose from. There is also a vast array of additives that can be used with paraffin wax in order to alter its nature to suit particular jobs (see pp. 20–1).

beeswax

Beeswax and paraffin wax are, in almost every respect, opposites, requiring very different methods to obtain good results. The most important difference is that, whereas paraffin wax can be heated quickly, beeswax must be coaxed up to temperature slowly—and never heated above 185°F (85°C)—or the color of the wax will spoil.

Molten beeswax has the viscous quality of cold vegetable oil, and as a result it demands an extra-thick wick. As it hardens, it grows gradually stiffer, until finally it is no longer pliable but is still a little sticky. This slow, steady setting curve means that you should always allow beeswax candles to cure for at least 24 hours—and, if you have time, preferably for a month—before using. Wrap in smooth tissue and store in a cool, dark place. The wax will harden to a beautiful

WAX TEMPERATURES

	100% paraffin wax	100% beeswax
Melting point	135–142°F (57–61°C)	144–147°F (62–64°C)
Priming wick	160°F (71°C)	169°F (76°C)
Container candles	160°F (71°C)	156°F (69°C)
Rigid molds	180–199°F (82–93°C)	149–158°F (65–70°C)
Flexible molds	180–185°F (82–85°C)	149–158°F (65–70°C)
Dipping	160°F (71°C)	156–160°F (69–71°C)
Overdipping/final dip	180°F (82°C)	162°F (72°C)
Clear overdip	205°F (96°C)	N/A
Pouring	160–180°F (71–82°C)	149–167°F (65–75°C)
Ice candles	210°F (99°C)	N/A
Balloon candles	180°F (82°C)	N/A
Wax inclusions	151°F (66°C)	151°F (66°C)
Adding perfume	151–158°F (66–70°C)	149–158°F (65–70°C)

glossy shine. Should a dusty bloom develop, simply wipe with a soft cloth.

Natural beeswax has properties that paraffin wax needs additives to emulate. First, it is ideal for use in container candles, thanks to its slow cooling and built-in stickiness. Second, its great tensile strength means that it is the material of choice for large and elaborate dipped or poured projects. If dropped, a beeswax candle will dent at the point of impact, while a paraffin candle would shatter.

Another factor in its favor is that beeswax no longer counts as a luxury—if you order directly from the beekeeper, it can be much cheaper than the petrochemical alternative.

The natural scent of beeswax is more intoxicating than any manmade perfume, and beeswax candles burn far longer and more sweetly than any alternative. Buy beeswax in chunks or foundation sheets, or as candle-making pellets in chemically bleached or natural forms.

wicks and additives

There is a range of products that can be added to paraffin wax. Adding 5% beeswax to paraffin wax increases burning time, while 5–25% produces shades ranging from ivory to vanilla.

PICK THE RIGHT WICK

ratio of paraffin to beeswax in candle

standard wick size (inches)	100% paraffin wax	80:20	60:40	50:50	40:60	20:80	100% beeswax
½	⅝	½	⅜	⅜	⅜	¼	¼
1	1	¾	¾	¾	¾	⅝	½
1½	1½	1¼	1⅛	1⅛	1	⅞	¾
2	2	1¾	1⅝	1½	1⅜	1¼	1
2½	2⅝	2⅜	2⅛	2	1¾	1⅝	1½
3	3	2¾	2½	2¼	2	1¾	1½
3½	3½	3⅛	2¾	2¾	2½	2	1⅞
4	4	3½	3⅛	2⅞	2¾	2½	2

Suitable for candles of roughly these dimensions (inches)

This chart shows you how to match your wick size to the appropriate candle size, according to the ratio of paraffin to beeswax in your candle. The actual diameter consumed by a wick will vary according to many factors, so experiment until you settle on the ideal wick size.

wicks

Wick sizes refer to the diameter of the finished candle and apply only to 100% paraffin wax candles. For a 100% beeswax candle, choose a wick recommended for at least twice its diameter (see chart for wax blends and p. 34 for extra-thick wicks). Braided cotton wicks are the most common and should always be primed before use (see p. 28). Container wicks consist of cotton braided cord formed around a rigid core. Also requiring priming,

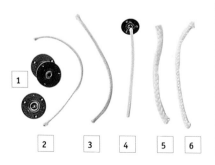

1. Sustainers
2. Container wick with metal core
3. Container wick with paper core
4. Jelly wax wick
5. 2-inch braided wick
6. 1-inch braided wick
7. Regular candle makers can buy economical rolls

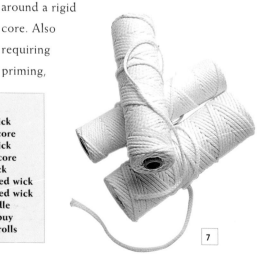

they should be used with sustainers (see pp. 36–7). Floating candle and jelly wax wicks are encased in a thick outer covering of paraffin wax, so there is no need to prime.

microcrystalline soft wax

This gives paraffin wax the stickiness of beeswax, preventing it from pulling away from the sides of containers. It is the principal ingredient in modeling wax (see additives chart).

microcrystalline hard wax

This can be used as an overdip to give candles a lacy outer shell, or added to paraffin wax in tiny quantities to improve burning time and finish. It also increases structural strength.

Melt it over direct heat to 199°F (93°C) and add it slowly to the molten paraffin wax.

plastic additive

This is used in quantities of 5% or less to increase burning time and improve appearance. Melt over direct heat to 219°F (104°C) and add slowly to the molten wax.

stearin

Stearin is added to paraffin wax to maximize shrinkage during molding, produce a glossy finish, and improve burning. The proportions should be 10% stearin to 90% wax. Never use stearin in a flexible mold because it will destroy the rubber; use Vybar instead.

PARAFFIN WAX ADDITIVES

Quantities given here take 100% to be the total amount of blended wax you are making, e.g. for modelling wax, add 70g microcrystalline soft to every 30g paraffin wax, plus 1g or more of petroleum jelly.

KEY
italic additives to be used in combination
• can be used in any proportion
† alternatives

	microcrystalline soft wax	microcrystalline hard wax	stearin	vybar	plastic additive	beeswax	petroleum jelly	candle perfume/ essential oils	candle dyes	natural pigments
container candles	10%†					•†		•	•	No
modeling wax	70%*					100%†	1%+ *	No	•	No
water candles					1%	No	No		•	•
ice candles					1%	No	•		•	•
rigid molds		1–5%	10%			•		•	•	No
flexible molds		No		0.5%		•		No	•	No
dipping			10%			•		No	•	No
overdipping		1%†	10%†			•		No	•	•
special effects		•	•			•		•	•	•
jelly wax	N/A	N/A	N/A	N/A	N/A	N/A	N/A	No	No	No

utensils

Apart from a few special items, all the equipment you need to make beautiful candles is somewhere in your kitchen already. Adapt all kinds of vessels to make molds, or dip short tapers in a catering-size tin can.

melting

Wax must be heated in a container placed over a second container filled with water, which stands on the heat source. A purpose made double boiler is ideal, but an old 4-piece camp cookery set is a low-cost alternative. Use the two saucepans as a large double boiler, and the lids for a miniature version.

Alternately, old tin cans work well, and if you pinch a little spout into the side of each one, they can be used for pouring, too. A candle maker's thermometer is also essential. Place the bulb of the thermometer in the molten wax to be sure of an accurate reading, then wipe it clean with paper towels while the wax is liquid. Pour leftover molten wax into flexible plastic containers. Once set, the wax chunks can simply be popped out for storage.

dipping

You will need a dipping can and a large water bath in which to stand it. A stockpot like the one shown is ideal. Remember the deeper the dipping can sits in the water, the better your candles will be. Hooks or wooden battens for hanging the dipped candles while they cool are required, as well as a sink of cold water for plunging the candles following the final dip.

Molds: The clear plastic molds pictured here are made in rigid polycarbonate. This material is the most economical route to versatility and strength. You can also get cheaper plastic, and more expensive metal and glass molds. Whichever sort of mold you choose, always make sure you have weights to hand before filling the mold with wax, otherwise you will find it will float to the top of the water bath.

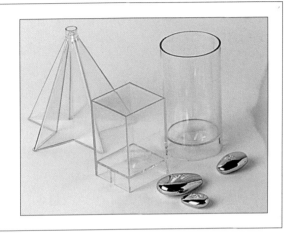

molding

You will need a wicking needle, skewers, and putty-like mold seal to prepare the molds. A container or sink full of warm or cold water is then required in which to submerge the filled mold, plus a weight to hold it down. If using beeswax or flexible molds, you will also need mold release. Spray silicone is best, but a 50:50 mix of liquid detergent and glycerin will do. If you are using the detergent/glycerin mix, allow it to dry before pouring the candle.

1. **Purpose made double boiler**
2. **4-piece camp cookery set**
3. **Old tin cans with pinched spouts**
4. **Wicking needle**
5. **Dipping can**
6. **Stockpot**

basic techniques

rolling

For a quick, easy, and satisfying way to start candle making, try rolling your own. All you need are readymade sheets of honey-comb-patterned beeswax, available in a rainbow of colors.

Beeswax foundation sheets are readily available from bee-keeping suppliers and craft stores. In the latter, they are available natural and dyed. All you need is a sharp knife, a cutting mat, a steel ruler, a source of gentle dissipated heat, and wick ¾–1¼" (2–3cm) longer than the finished candle. The great advantage of rolling candles is that you only need to melt a drop of wax to prime the wick. You could use an unprimed wick, but the burning quality of the candle will be poorer.

1 Make sure that your work surface is completely clean because beeswax sheets are sticky even before they are warmed, and they will pick up any dust or fiber they can find. Cut the sheet of wax to the profile you plan to

use. The shape shown below produces a long, tapered profile. For a flat-topped candle, cut a rectangle (see pp. 48–9). For a beehive-shaped mound, cut a long, thin strip with one side running down the length of the strip at a shallow angle (see templates opposite). To give a neat finish around the wick on a steeply sloping taper, leave ½" (1–1.5cm) of straight edge before beginning to cut the angle. Choose the wick carefully (see p. 20).

2 Melt a little beeswax in a small pouring can to the appropriate temperature (see p. 19). While waiting, use a hair dryer to warm the wax sheet evenly all over, or put it in a warm place for a few minutes, such as near a radiator. You want to soften the sheet so that it is

soft, sticky, and limp, but not so much that it begins to melt and lose its shape. Lay the sheet back down on the work surface. Once the wax in the can has melted, prime the wick (see p. 28). While the wax is still liquid, quickly transfer the wick to the wider edge of the wax sheet, stretch it out as shown, and stick it to the sheet by gently running your hand along its length to smooth it down.

3 Making sure that the wax sheet is still pliable, gently tease the edge of the wax around the wick, ensuring that it is properly aligned. Start to push gently against the wax sheet with your fingertips, working up and down the length of the candle so that the sheet is rolled evenly from top to bottom. Once you have completed a couple of turns, roll the remainder of the sheet around the candle with a couple of sweeps of your hands. When finished, press gently down the edge on the side of the candle in order to stick the sheet firmly in place.

4 To prevent the candle from coming apart when cold, you can planish to even the base and seal the wax layers together using the warm, flat surface of an iron. Alternatively, gently heat a pan on the stove and rub the candle base across the hot surface.

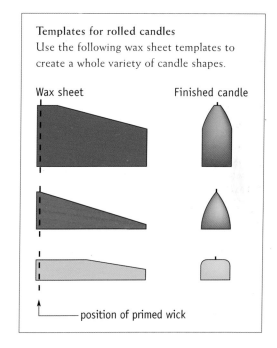

Templates for rolled candles
Use the following wax sheet templates to create a whole variety of candle shapes.

Wax sheet   Finished candle

position of primed wick

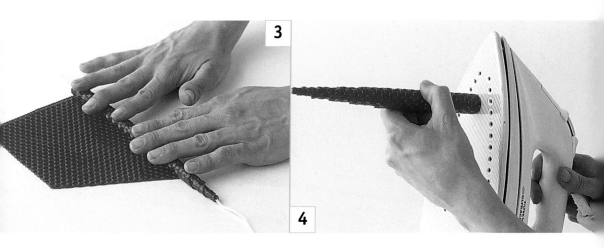

3

4

dipping

There is a soporific rhythm to dipping that calms the mind and unknots the muscles, giving you the ultimate stress release in a single afternoon. As a bonus, in the material world dipping also yields some beautiful candles.

Ensure that there are no drafts and the room is evenly warm, or the candles will bend as they cool. Two candles can be dipped at once using a doubled length of wick. When finished, hang the loops of wick over S-hooks suspended from half-opened drawers while the candles set. Alternately, cut grooves in a strip of wood and press the wicks into the grooves. The wood strip can then be supported between two chairs to dry.

1 First, prime the wick. Fill a dipping can with wax melted to the appropriate temperature (see p. 19), then turn the heat down. Cut the wicks to length, then submerge in the hot wax for up to a minute, until no more bubbles can be seen escaping from the braid.

2 Draw the wick out of the wax when soaked, wait until it stops dripping, then draw it taut until it stiffens. Dip twice more to complete the priming stage.

3 Check that the wax is at the correct temperature for dipping (see p. 19), then dip the primed wick several times until you have sticks of about ¼" (5mm) across. Periodically check the temperature of the wax while you are working, and reheat as required. Dip to around ½" (1cm) shorter than the primed wick for classic tapers, though you can make some interesting profiles by varying the depth to which you dip. If you are dipping lots of candles, work in rotation. If you are doing a single pair, wait 30 seconds between dips. Keep a reservoir of heated wax at hand to refill the dipping can as necessary, keeping the depth of wax in the can around 1¼" (3cm) deeper than the length of the candles.

4 Regularly trim the drip (known as the port) that forms at the bottom of the candles using strong scissors. Do this with the candles hanging. Stop dipping just before they achieve the diameter you want, trim the port neatly, then dip once or twice more. For a glossy finish, you may want to increase the temperature of the wax for the final dip. Plunge the warm candles into cold water and leave them there to set.

molding

Molding is the most popular method for making candles at home, and it is not hard to figure out why. As long as you observe some basic technical rules, you can be guaranteed to produce a great candle every time.

1 Melt the wax slowly in a double boiler, then prime the wick (see p. 28). Use mold release if required (see p. 23). Thread the wick through the hole in the base of the mold, then push a wicking needle or skewer through the wick to support it at the top. Ensure it is centrally positioned, and pull it taut. Glue the wick into its hole with mold seal.

When the wax reaches the correct temperature (see p. 19), fill the mold to about ½" (1cm) from the top. Wait a second or two, then give it a couple of firm taps to remove any air bubbles that may have formed.

2 If using paraffin wax, fill a container with cold water to half the height of the mold. Put the mold into this cold water bath, weight it

down, and add more water until it is level with the height of the wax. Leave for 10–30 minutes, until a skin has formed over the top of the wax and the center of the candle has sunk down to form a well around the wick.

3 Use a wicking needle or skewer to break the skin around the wick and refill with wax to the original level. Allow to cool, then repeat the skin-popping and refilling until no well forms. Allow to set for anything from an hour to overnight, depending on size. If using beeswax, put the mold into warm water instead, and leave in place overnight. It is unusual to have to refill a beeswax candle because of its slow cooling.

4 Remove the mold seal, and the candle should slip out easily. If stuck, put it in the refrigerator for half an hour or so, then try again. Planish the bottom (see p. 27).

Calculating wax quantities
Block the wick hole and fill the mold with water to the desired level. Decant the water into a measuring cup or jug to find out the liquid quantity of wax required. To make $3\frac{1}{4}$fl oz (100ml) of liquid wax, melt about $2\frac{3}{4}$oz (80g) of solid wax. If using paraffin wax, this figure needs to be broken down into 90% paraffin wax and 10% stearin.

making molds

There is nothing more exciting than making your own candle from scratch, including the mold. Adapt all sorts of vessels from around the house, or use latex to create fabulous molds from just about anything you can get your hands on.

Choosing objects for molds

Ordinary household items, such as mixing bowls, cake tins, and pastry cutters, can all be used as molds. You can also shape heavyweight aluminum foil or strong cardboard into single-use molds. The only rules are that the open end of the mold must be the same size as, or bigger than, the bottom, and have no undulations along its sides, or the set candle will be trapped inside. Alternately, you can buy a kit of liquid latex and setting additive to create a flexible mold. The list of items you can use as a form for your mold is endless—pieces of fresh fruit, beautifully shaped stones and fossils, favorite ornaments, interestingly shaped ceramics, or even baby toys and rubber ducks! If you are using something not immediately suitable for mold making, a bottle for instance, plug the hole with modeling clay and paint the latex over it.

1 Choose the object you'd like to use as a form. Here we've used a lemon because of its pleasing shape and interesting texture. Fruit dye disks and scent can be added for a really fruity effect! To make it easier to pour wax into the finished mold add some modeling clay to the form where the base of the candle will be. This extra bulk will create a funnel

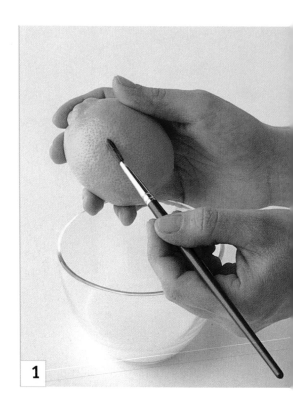

1

neck for pouring in wax. Following the manufacturer's instructions, coat the form with releasing agent (usually washing detergent) and then coat the form with the mixture of latex compound and setting agent using a fine brush. Make sure you work the mixture into all the contours of the form and build up the mold in layers, ensuring each one is fully dry before applying the next.

2 When you have built up enough layers and the latex is completely dry, peel the mold off the form, wash out any debris with tap water, and allow it to dry. Use a wicking needle to thread a primed wick (see p. 28) through the mold. Suspend the top of the wick from the needle or skewer, and seal the hole at the bottom of the mold with mold seal.

3 Use flexible molds in the same way as rigid ones (see pp. 30–1), but use Vybar instead of stearin when making a paraffin wax candle, and reduce the temperature of the wax (see p. 19). You also need to support the mold while making the candle. Once it is full, pinch the mold to remove bubbles rather than tapping it. When the candle has set, peel off the mold. It is easiest to remove the candle before it is completely cold. Use mold release with either beeswax or paraffin wax, and you may find it helpful to lubricate the outside of the mold when you turn it inside out.

pouring

If you have a strong sense of adventure, pouring is the technique for you. It is a skill that takes some mastering, but is the only way you can make floor-standing sculptures. Even if you lack the urge to make enormous candles, pouring can be used instead of overdipping in many cases.

Whatever scale you decide on, always make sure that you have a really strong anchor point from which to suspend the wick, for the candle will grow surprisingly heavy. For very large candles, you'll need a ladder, and a stout hook. The other equipment you'll need includes: plenty of wick, a large double boiler, lots of old newspapers, and a small hand-bowl or pouring tin or can—but the most important thing you will need is lots of practice. For smaller candles, you could suspend the wick by hand, but you will still need a strong hook so that you can hang the finished candle to cool.

1

2

1 Decide the diameter of the finished candle and choose an appropriately sized wick (see p. 20). For large candles, you may need to braid several wicks together to achieve an appropriate thickness to consume the candle properly. Knot the wicks at the top, suspend from a hook, and braid tightly and evenly. Allow around 50% extra length when cutting the three pieces of wick to take into account the twists of the plait. Even if you are using a single wick, allow an extra length of 6" (15cm).

2 For a really long candle, you will need to use a portable stove on the floor. Spread out plenty of newspapers, put the stove on these, then set the wax to melt in a double boiler to the appropriate temperature (see p. 19). Prime the wick (see p. 28).

3 Fill a pouring can with wax and hold it next to the top of the wick. Hold the wick between the fingers of your other hand, and roll it gently back and forth between them so that it spins. Once the wick is spinning well, pour the molten wax down it. The more regularly and quickly the wick spins, the better the finished candle. Allow to cool between pours, rolling it between your palms to straighten it. Smooth the surface at intervals. Continue in this way, adding more molten wax to the pouring can as necessary, until the fattest point of the candle has reached your ideal diameter.

3

Finishing techniques

There are several ways you can turn the giant wax cucumber you are left with at the end of the pouring process into an attractive candle. The traditional method is as follows: lay the poured candle on a flat surface while still a little warm, and use a sharp knife to cut through the bottom of the candle until a length of wick ½" (1cm) is revealed. Pick up the candle by this wick, so the candle is reversed, hold it over the double boiler, and pour wax over its surface until you achieve a parallel-sided pillar. Finish by trimming and planishing the new base (see p. 27). Alternatively, to create a candle with a thin, tapered point, simply slice off the base and planish the surface. Then trim the excess wick at the top.

container candles

If you crave a feast of fragrance you'll love container candles. They are easy to make—just add essential oils to the melted wax before pouring it into the container—and extremely versatile. Choose containers in any shape and size, that suit your interior.

Making container candles is similar to molding, but for container candles, blend 10% microcrystalline soft wax with the paraffin wax rather than stearin. Micro-crystalline soft prevents the wax from coming away from the sides of the container; stearin has the opposite effect. If you wish, add essential oils as outlined on p. 44.

1 Choose container candle wick of a suitable size (see p. 20), plus a corresponding wick sustainer. Always use a wick whose melt pool is smaller than the diameter of the pot you are using. Prime the wick (see p. 28) and attach the sustainer using pliers—electrician's wire cutters are ideal. They have three crimp-er slots for attaching terminals to electric wires, so put the sustainer into the slot best suited to its size, feed the wick through the hole, then close the crimpers to hold it firmly in place. (You can buy wicks with sustainers attached, but they are not widely available.) Trim the wick flush with the bottom of the sustainer and about $\frac{3}{4}$" (2cm) longer than the height of the container. Mix some epoxy resin glue and stick the sustainer centrally in the bottom of the container.

2 When the glue has hardened, secure the top of the wick in a central position. For

larger candles, knot string around the wick, then use masking tape to stick the string to the edges of the container with the wick upright. Wicks for smaller candles can be propped up as in molding (see p. 30). You can keep the wick vertical in tiny candles with just a piece of masking tape, as shown here. Melt your wax blend to the appropriate temperature (see p. 19), then pour it slowly and carefully into the container. Stop pouring around ¼" (5mm) short of the candle's eventual height, reserving enough wax for one or two refills. Allow the candle to cool.

3 When the candle has cooled, pour in the reserved wax, making sure that the new layer covers the first and reaches the container sides. With a tiny candle, this should be the end of the pouring process. With larger candles you may have to refill several times.

4 When the candle is cold, remove the wick props, trim the wick to length, and enjoy.

Choosing containers

If using a glass container, set it in a bath of hot water to ensure that it is thoroughly warmed before you pour in the molten wax. Try to match the temperature of the glass to that of the wax if you can. This does more than simply protect against cracks. It also prevents ridges from forming as the wax flows in, and stops the wax from cooling too rapidly and pulling away from the sides, spoiling the look and distorting the color. This is not important when using an opaque container, because the look of the candle's top is your only concern. Just be sure to keep the wax as cool as possible when pouring to avoid cracking fragile ceramics. Always set containers on a thick wad of newspaper, regardless of the material they are made of, in case of spills or leaks caused by the warmth of the wax. Plenty of old galvanized tinware will spring a leak with only the slightest provocation.

jelly wax

This amazing transparent jelly can be used alone, with inclusions, or in combination with other waxes. Using jelly wax chunks as inclusions in a candle molded in either beeswax or paraffin wax produces a remarkable, vibrant mosaic effect.

1 Jelly wax uses a one-size-fits-all wick, pre-coated in paraffin wax. Attach a sustainer if it does not already have one, and glue to the base of the container (see p. 36). (Alternatively, pour the candle first, pierce the wax with a wicking needle and insert the wick.) Arrange inclusion materials, ensuring that they are a safe distance from the wick.

2 Melt the wax together with any color in a double boiler, to 203°F (95°C). You may find it easier to place it in an oven instead. Do not let any water splash into the wax, or it will turn cloudy. Concentrated pigments may be available for use with jelly wax, and should be added to the melted wax in a proportion of 0.1–0.2%. You can also get

1

2

predyed wax, that can be added to melted plain jelly wax.

3 Support the wick (see pp. 36–7), and pour a little wax into the bottom of the container to hold the inclusions steady. Allow this to set, reposition any inclusions that have moved, then refill to ¾" (2cm) below the rim. Pour slowly to avoid creating too many bubbles. In larger candles, pour the wax in layers, inserting additional inclusions once each layer has cooled. For the candle shown here, retain a little wax, remove it from the heat, and allow it to set.

4 Add pieces of spare wax on the top of the candle, ensuring the wick has room to breathe.

Safety considerations

Any heatproof vessel or dishwasher-safe glass container is suitable for use with jelly wax. Place it on a heatproof surface because it can get quite hot. Do not use plastic materials—they may melt when the candle is poured. Either space inclusions well away from the wick at the base of the candle, or insert a wick only to a depth where the candle will be extinguished before it reaches the decoration. Jelly wax is slightly toxic, so wash your hands after use.

surface decoration

The simplest candle can be transformed into a decorative feature with a little surface decoration. Use general craft techniques with wax or other materials for a fabulous and professional finish.

appliqué

Wax appliqué is an easy and effective technique. Make millefiori canes from modeling wax (see p. 86), or cut a design from readymade appliqué wax sheets. They come in a fabulous array of colors and are self-adhesive.

1 Cut out the design with the wax still attached to its backing paper. To interleave different colored sections, work as in marquetry, lying the various sheets on top of one another and cutting through the stack to ensure that the pieces fit together.

2 Apply the wax pieces to the candle, gently pressing in place until your design is perfect. Once you are happy with the positioning, apply heavier pressure to attach them firmly.

3 To achieve a level edge use a sharp knife to trim any overhang top and bottom.

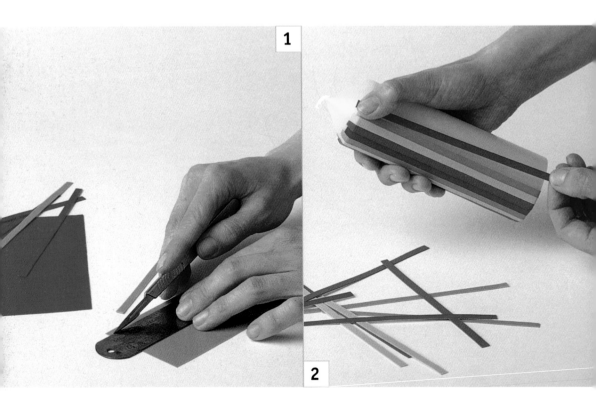

4 Melt some paraffin wax in a dipping can to 205°F (96°C). Submerge the candle for a couple of seconds, allow it to cool for 30 seconds, then dip it briefly a second time. This overdip seals in the appliquéd design.

gilding

Apply gold leaf directly onto newly dipped candles, then use a burnishing tool to trace the design. On a cold candle, apply gilding size and then apply the leaf. For a speckled effect, mask off areas you do not want to gild, then apply a light drift of spray glue. For both these techniques, finish by rubbing down the leaf with a soft tissue.

marbling

Float little drifts of color on the surface of water (hot for waxes, cold for alcohol-based glass paints), then dip the candle through the colored layer. You can also achieve a similar effect by sprinkling powdered candle dye onto the surface of a finished candle, then wafting a blowtorch over the powder to heat it gently.

pressed flowers

A pressed-flower design can be applied by simply gluing the flowers to the candle using strong, undiluted wood glue. If all the flowers are completely flat, overdipping will complete the design beautifully.

adding color

You can use any wax-soluble substance to create candles with technicolor eye appeal, from wax crayons to mineral pigments, although purpose made candle dye disks are the most reliable and convenient. For a real rainbow of wax colors, mix your own blends for fun.

mineral pigments

Melt 3½oz (100g) of plain wax in an old can, then add up to ¼oz (10g) of pigment, depending on the color you want to achieve. Stir well, leave on a low heat for an hour or so, allow it to set, remelt it, then stir it again and pour it into a flexible plastic container into which you have already poured a little hot water. Let it cool slowly. When it sets, pop the colored wax out of the container and scrape away the blanched particles from the bottom of the block. Store it for future use.

powder dyes

Commercial candle makers use powdered wax dyes, generally available in quantities to dye 500lb (250kg) of wax at a time. Their inclusion in recipes is usually at around 1% of the total weight of wax, except for chalky white (titanium dioxide), which needs to be used in a far greater concentration, sometimes nearer 20%. Some powder colors are difficult to dissolve, so use at least 1% stearin and melt the color separately from the main wax reservoir, ensuring that it is dissolved before putting the two together.

Natural mineral pigments are exciting to use because no two batches of dyed wax will ever be the same. Always test a new blend as an overdip before using it as the body of a candle, because some pigments will not burn willingly.

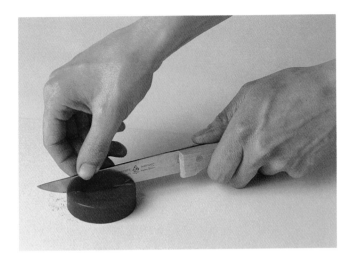

A whole dye disk will color 4½ lb (2kg) of wax, so cut it into appropriate portions for smaller quantities—half a disk for 2¼ lb (1kg) of wax, a quarter disk for 17½ oz (500g), an eighth for 8½ oz (250g), and a sixteenth for 3½ oz (100g). Shave off a few curls for pastel shades.

dye disks

Dye disks are little blocks of colored stearin and wax, so in most cases they will dissolve successfully in a vat of plain molten wax without any additives, though sometimes you will need to dissolve them in some stearin first (follow the manufacturer's instructions). The one disk color that is hard to use is pearly white (see box). As a rough guide, each dye disk will color around 4½ lb (2kg) of wax to the intensity shown on the label. When using dye disks in very small amounts it is best to measure according to ratios between colors. In the recipes featured in this book we refer to parts, for instance, 1 part blue to 2 parts yellow will produce a light green color.

Trouble with whites

Pearly white dye disk and chalky white powder dye can be difficult to use, so follow the recommendations below.

• Chalky white—Never use this for the body of a candle because it does not burn well. Use it to color wax for molding around a core candle or for overdipping.

• Pearly white—This is harder to melt than other dye disks. Shave the disk into little curls, melt them separately from the main bulk of wax and any other colors, and at a higher than usual temperature. Pour in a little of the main wax, swirl it around until the two have blended, then pour the mix back into the main melting pot.

Each of these wax domes was made using the same amount of the same fuchsia dye. Can you spot the difference? The one on the right is of pure beeswax, while that on the left is a paraffin/stearin blend.

adding scent

Perfume is the finishing touch for any candle. Change the atmosphere of your home, extinguish bad smells or repel bugs in the garden—all by the subtle use of aromatic inclusions, readymade candle perfumes, or aromatherapist's essential oils.

aromatic inclusions

Whole spice or gum inclusions, such as grains of frankincense or myrrh, or lumps of gum benzoin, produce beautifully fragrant candles. Whole spice pieces, such as star anise, dried root ginger, cinnamon sticks, and vanilla pods, can be molded into a candle, then carved around to give a deep relief look.

candle perfume

Candle-making suppliers offer a wide range of perfumes designed for adding to hot wax. Use 1tsp (5ml) of perfume for 2¼lb (1kg) of wax. Add the fragrance when the wax is as cool as possible (see p. 19).

essential oils

Use essential oils to scent container candles or those formed using glass, aluminum, or rigid polycarbonate molds. Do not work with oils if you are pregnant or breast-feeding. Only use pure essential oils, never carrier oils because they will spoil the candles. Add the oil when the wax is as cool as possible (see p. 19). Use 10–40 drops of oil for every 5½oz/7fl oz (160g/200ml) of wax. An eye dropper from a drug store is indispensable for adding large quantities of oil—20 drops make a fifth of a teaspoon (1ml).

For a fresh citrus aroma, choose essential oil of orange, lime, lemon, or mandarin. Lime and mandarin give a sweeter fragrance than the others.

Choosing essential oils

Mix oils from more than one mood group for a complex effect, or combine by season.

• Relaxing: *Geranium, sandalwood, clary sage, frankincense, jasmine, ylang-ylang, chamomile, lavender*
• Stimulating: *Grapefruit, melissa, mandarin, orange, coriander, cardamom, ginger, black pepper, lemon, nutmeg, hyssop, lime, thyme*
• Sultry: *Benzoin resinoid, vanilla, patchouli, oakmoss, tonka bean, ylang-ylang, jasmine, sandalwood*
• Spring: *Palmarosa, geranium, rosewood, camphor, fennel, angelica, grapefruit, lime, melissa, petitgrain, thyme*
• Summer: *Vanilla, sandalwood, basil, ginger, jasmine, lavender, lemon, lemongrass, marjoram, geranium, rosemary, peppermint*
• Fall: *Cedar, cypress, orange, mandarin, melissa, verbena, benzoin resinoid, patchouli, sandalwood, vetiver, bergamot, spikenard*
• Winter: *Cinnamon, clove, orange, mandarin, bay, cedar, pine, frankincense, myrrh, benzoin resinoid, juniper*

vapor lamp

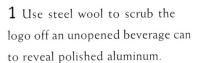

A vapor lamp is a little dish, suspended over a tea light flame, in which drops of oil are floated on a pool of water.

1 Use steel wool to scrub the logo off an unopened beverage can to reveal polished aluminum.

2 Empty the can, then use strong scissors to cut out a window for the candle to be inserted. Apply a strip of self-adhesive metal foil over the cut edge, then carefully punch a pattern of holes over the can's surface with a scissor point.

3 Use air dry modeling clay to level and weight the base of the lamp, both inside and out. Allow to dry, then glue if necessary.

4 Score the foiled backs of several frosted glass cabochon beads, apply a tiny amount of glue around the larger holes on the can, then press the beads into place. Allow the glue to set completely before using the lamp.

pure and
simple

honey sticks

These simple candles can be made with very little
equipment and no fuss. Natural beeswax foundation sheets
are available from candle-making or bee-keeping suppliers,
and rolling them into sweet-smelling candles is a wonderful
way to relax.

one Beeswax sheets are available in two depths. The
deeper variety is used for making candles and is called a
brood sheet. It usually measures 8 x 13½" (20 x 34cm).
When buying sheets from a beekeeper, ask for unwired
brood foundation. For this project the fat candle is made
from a whole sheet, rolled along its shorter edge, and has
a 1¾" (4.5cm) diameter. The three thin candles are
made from a second sheet of wax, cut widthways into
three lengths: one 5½" (14cm) and two 4" (10cm).
When they are rolled along their shorter edges each has
a diameter of ¾" (2cm). Calculate the wick dimensions
you require (see p. 20). **two** Cut the sheets to the
required size and cut a slope along one side if you want
tapered candles (see p. 27). **three** Melt the wax to the
appropriate temperature (see p. 19) and prime the wicks
(see p. 28). Warm and roll the sheets (see pp. 26–7).
Planish the base of the candles (see p. 27).

---

utensils

Steel ruler • Sharp knife • Small double
boiler • Old iron or frying pan
• Hair dryer

ingredients

Natural beeswax foundation sheets •
Suitable wicks • 3½ oz (100g) paraffin
wax or beeswax

Opposite: *These simple but beautiful
candles are made from natural beeswax,
but most candle-making suppliers also
sell sheets in a wild array of colors if
you would prefer to make a more
exciting and dramatic statement.*

coco cabana

Transform your summer terrace into a Caribbean beach with an array of coconut shells, each glimmering with the light of a built-in candle. Scent cunningly with vanilla and cedar perfumes for a convincing coconut aroma.

one For a coconut without a husk, stretch a rubber band around it to mark the cutting line and saw it in half. Discard the pointed top half and file a flat area on the rounded base. If the coconut has its husk, slice through the husk along the cutting line with a serrated knife, then saw in half. Use the knife to slice off a flat bottom area. Clean the shell thoroughly. two Calculate how much wax you will need to fill the shell to ¾" (2cm) below the rim (see p. 31), and set the blend, minus the perfumes, to melt (see pp. 42–3 regarding colors). three Prime the wick (see p. 28). Attach the sustainer, glue it into the base of the shell, and support the wick at the top of the shell with string and masking tape (see pp. 36–7). Stand the prepared shell in a cup to keep it upright. four Once the wax has stabilized at 160°F (71°C), add the perfumes and carefully pour it into the shell. The shell's absorbency means that any splashed wax will leave a stain when scraped away. Allow to cool. five Once the wax has set sufficiently to create a well, use a wicking needle to pierce the wax beside the wick, then refill (see p. 37). On your final pour, flow the wax right to the edges of the shell, and allow to cool completely before removing the wick supports.

utensils

Whole coconut • Rubber band • Hacksaw • Coarse file • Large serrated knife • Double boiler • Pliers • String • Masking tape • Cup • Wicking needle

ingredients

Large container candle wick • Wick sustainer • Epoxy resin glue • Paraffin wax, plus the following ingredients for every 3½ oz (100g) of wax: ¾ oz (20g) microcrystalline soft wax, shavings of cream dye disk, 1/32 oz (1g) pearly white dye disk, 8 drops vanilla candle perfume, and 4 drops cedar candle perfume

Opposite: *Take extra care when burning these candles because coconut shell and husk are both flammable. If the wick ever touches the side of the shell, extinguish the candle immediately.*

multiwicked slab

An ordinary cake tin makes the perfect mold for this slab
candle, which combines the simplicity of contemporary
minimalism with the soulful flames of candlelight. You will
need to work in a warm, draft-free room to make this candle
because a water bath is not used.

utensils

Double boiler • 8" (20cm) cake tin with
removable base (removed) • Sheet of glass
• Mold seal • Shallow 8" (20cm)
diameter heatproof container • Pair of
dividers or compass • Steel ruler • Strong
scissors • Wicking needle • Cork • Gas
burner or blowtorch

ingredients

2¾ lb (1.2kg) paraffin wax • 4¼ oz
(120g) beeswax • 4¼ oz (120g) stearin
• 1yd (1m) of 2" (5cm) container
candle wick

Opposite: *When inserting the wicks,
take care not to put too much pressure on
the wicking needle, since this will produce
white bruises on the surface of the wax
and spoil the finished look.*

one Melt the wax blend to 180°F (82°C). While
waiting, place the cake tin on the glass sheet and seal
firmly with mold seal. Place the shallow container with
hot water underneath the glass sheet directly under the
cake tin. **two** Prime the wick (see p. 28), then pour wax
into the cake tin mold and allow to set for 12 hours.
three Set the dividers or compass to 4" (10cm), place
one point at the edge of the mold, and scribe an arc
across the center of the wax. Move to the other side of
the mold and draw another arc. Where the arcs bisect is
the center point. **four** Draw a 2½" (6cm) radius circle
around this point. Place one point of the dividers
anywhere on the circle and scribe an arc across the circle
on one side. Move to the scribed mark and repeat, until
you have six scribed arcs. Pierce the intersections with
the dividers to mark the wicking positions. Remove the
candle from the mold. **five** Cut the wick into seven
lengths. Insert the eye of the wicking needle into a cork
and use it as a handle while heating the point of the
needle. Press the point against each of the pierced marks
so that it bores into the surface. As you do so, push a
length of wick through quickly. Twirl it as you insert it to
make the job easier. Reheat the needle as required. Trim
the wicks flush with the base of the candle and with ½"
(1cm) protruding from the top.

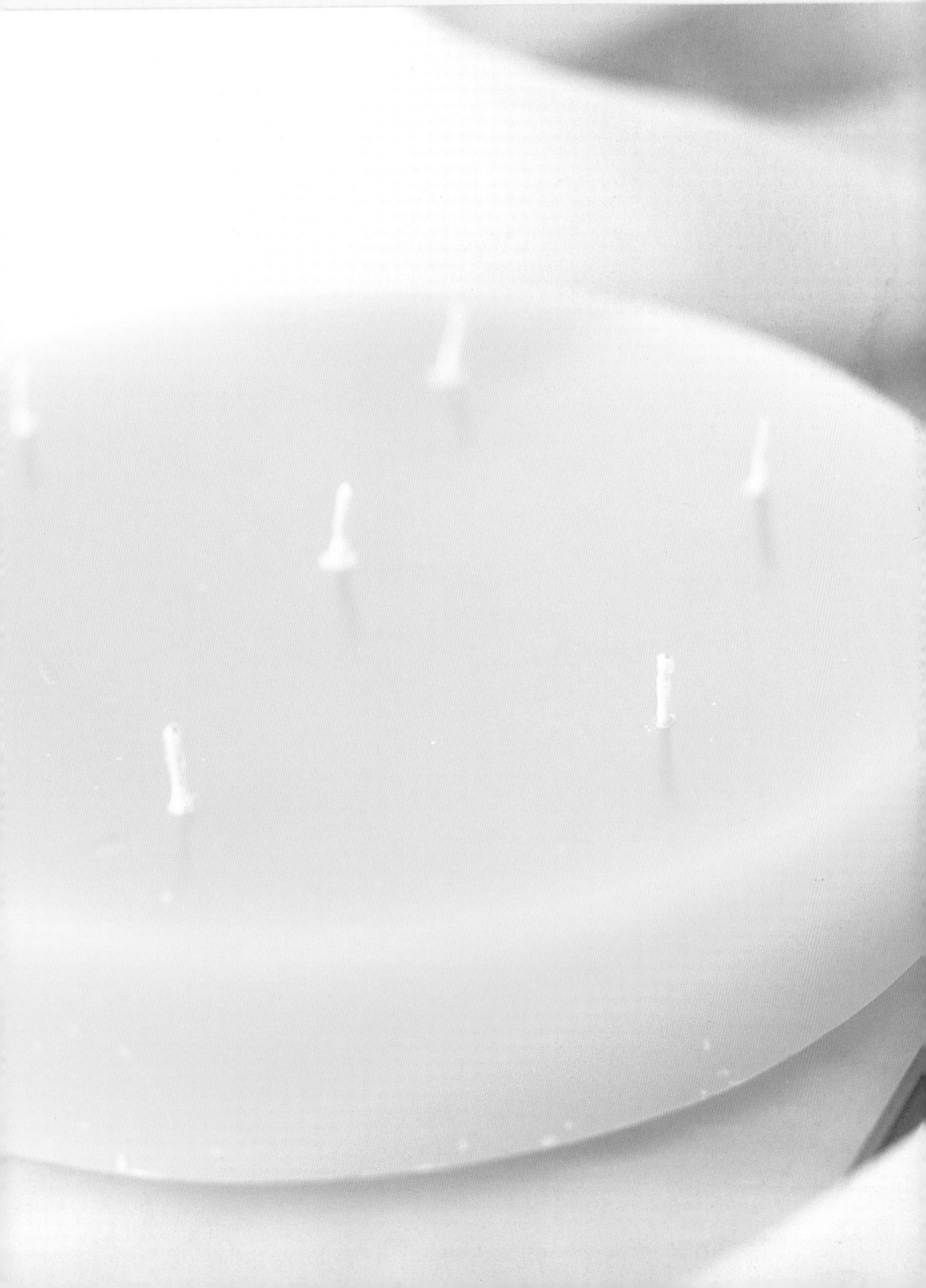

classic dips

Elegant, utilitarian, and utterly pure, the classic dipped beeswax taper is the aristocrat of candles, lending a timeless dignity to intimate natural light. The gentle rhythm of dipping purges stress while you are making them, too.

one Melt the wax slowly to 169°F (76°C) and prepare your means of hanging the candles (see p. 28). Cut 19½" (50cm) lengths of wick, fold double, and prime to a depth of 7½" (19cm) (see p. 28). Attach them to your hanging mechanism. **two** Place the dipping can in a stockpot of water on the stove, and fill with molten wax to a depth of 8¾" (22cm), taking care to retain its temperature. Dip the first doubled wick into the can and draw it out in one movement, pausing for a second or two at the bottom of the dip. **three** Continue to dip the candles and trim the ports from their bases (see pp. 28–9 for full instructions). Once the candles have begun to take form, measuring around ¼" (5mm) across, reduce the temperature of the wax to 156–160°F (69–71°C), then when the candles are just short of 1" (2.5cm) in diameter, increase the temperature to 161°F (72°C) for the final one or two dips. **four** Plunge the candles into the cold water bath. The hotter final dip followed by the cold water plunge gives the candles a smooth, glossy surface. **five** Trim the wicks to ½" (1cm), wrap the cold candles in smooth tissue, and store for at least 24 hours before lighting them.

utensils

Double boiler • Hanging books or wooden batons • Strong scissors • 10" (25cm) deep dipping can and stockpot • Cold water bath

ingredients

Beeswax • Skein of 1½ " (4cm) wick

Opposite: *Make sure that you submerge the candles to about the same depth each time you dip. This is important because it gives the candles their beautiful tapered profile.*

bursting into bloom

This delicate, egg-shaped candle is formed by dipping a balloon into different color waxes. The outer layer is then linocut with a design of flowers and polka dots to reveal the pink and blue layers beneath.

one Fill the balloon with cold water until it measures 4" (10cm) across, knot it and attach a string. **two** Melt dip 1 and pour some boiled water into the dipping can sufficiently deep to cover the balloon. Pour a ¾" (2cm) layer of molten wax on top. Stabilize the temperature at 180°F (82°C). **three** Dip three-quarters of the balloon into the can 20–30 times, refilling the wax pool as necessary (see pp. 28–9). Add the fuchsia dye to the wax pool and dip the balloon 5–10 times, then add blue and repeat. **four** Melt the overdip blend. Empty the dipping can, then pour in hot water and a pool of overdip. Stabilize the temperature at 180°F (82°C), then dip the candle until it is coated in opaque white. Hang the candle until it is hard but still warm. **five** Snip the neck of the balloon, empty the water, and remove the balloon. Support the dipped shell in a cup. **six** Melt the inner candle blend to 160°F (71°C). Prime the wick (see p. 28) and suspend it over the shell from a kabob stick. Add the white dye (see p. 43) and pour the wax into the shell ¾" (2cm) at a time, topping up as required. Leave overnight. **seven** Trim and chamfer the edge of the shell ¾" (2cm) above the main body. Use linocutters to carefully gouge out polka dots down to the blue layer, then gouge out six pink petals around one or two of the blue dots.

utensils

Round balloon • String • Two double boilers • Large, squat dipping can and stockpot • Sharp scissors • Hanging hook • Cup • Skewers • Wicking needle • Sharp knife • Linocutting set

ingredients

Dip 1: 7oz (200g) paraffin wax and ½oz (20g) stearin • Dips 2 and 3: Shavings of fuchsia dye disk and blue dye disk • Overdip: 3½oz (100g) paraffin wax, ¼ oz (10g) stearin, and ¼ tsp (1.25ml) chalky white powder dye • Inner candle: 8½ oz (250g) paraffin wax, 1oz (25g) stearin, and 1/16 pearly white dye disk • 8" (20cm) of 2" (5cm) wick

Opposite: *When finished this candle has a rounded base, so it must be firmly supported when lit. Stand it in a tea light or floating candle holder—or, alternatively, slice off a flat base at the carving stage.*

good enough
to eat

fruity columns

These fruity colored column candles are made using an inspired marbling technique. Make several shapes and sizes of candles in a couple of colors to produce a display that is nothing less than mouthwatering.

utensils

Double boiler • Pouring pitcher • Cold water bath • Paper towels • 12fl oz (350ml) capacity column mold • Wicking needle • Mold seal • Skewer • Weight • Old iron or frying pan

ingredients

1lb (450g) paraffin wax • 1¾ oz (50g) stearin • ¼ dye disk • 8" (20cm) of 2½" (6cm) wick • ½ tsp (2.5ml) fruity candle perfume or 10 drops essential oil

one Melt and color the wax blend (see pp. 42–3) and stabilize the temperature at 180°F (82°C). Prime the wick (see p. 28). Decant half the wax into the pouring pitcher, and switch off the heat. **two** Slowly pour the molten wax into the cold water bath. As it hits the water, it will form a wonderful, distorted cascade of glossy, frozen drizzles. **three** Scoop the wax pieces from the water, and dry thoroughly on paper towels. It is essential that all water is removed from these pieces or it will spoil the burning of the finished candle. Once perfectly dry, reheat the remainder of the wax blend. **four** While waiting, insert the wick into the mold, seal the hole, and support the top of the wick with a skewer (see pp. 30–1). Pack the mold with the wax drizzles. **five** Stabilize the temperature of the molten wax at 150°F (66°C), add the fragrance, then pour slowly into the mold. **six** Place the mold in the water bath, weight it down, and refill as required (see pp. 30–1). When set, planish the base (see p. 27).

Opposite: *Choose pink wax dye to go with strawberry candle perfume, pale green for a candle scented with lime essential oil, or make up your own combinations of color and fragrance for a tasty fresh and fruity look.*

good enough to eat

one fresh orange

Scented with sweet oil of mandarin, this exciting five-wicked orange candle will conjure images of summer on the most dreary winter day. Candy-colored wax and a special frosting technique combine to produce a candle that looks like orange sorbet.

one Calculate the capacity of the mixing bowl and wax quantities accordingly (see p. 31). Coat the bowl with mold release. Melt the wax blend for the second pouring in the large double boiler and add the dye (see pp. 42–3). Prime the wick (see p. 28) and keep the wax on a low heat. **two** Melt the wax blend for the first pouring in the small double boiler to 160°F (71°C), then carefully pour it around the walls of the bowl. Build up a ⅛" (3mm) layer, 1" (2.5cm) down from the rim. Immerse in the cold water bath until the wax becomes leathery. **three** Melt the second blend to 154–158°F (68–70°C), add the essential oils, and pour slowly into the bowl up to the level of the first coating. Place in the water bath, weighted and supported (crossed wooden rulers work well), and allow to set. **four** Refill the candle every time the surface becomes leathery and concave (see pp. 30–1). On the final refill, flow the wax over the whole surface to a depth of ¼" (5mm). Return to the water bath. **five** Once the candle is set but slightly warm, place the mold near a heat source. Use a wicking needle to mark the points for the wick holes and insert the wicks (see p. 52). Trim each wick to about 1¼" (3cm) above the surface of the candle. Return to the water bath, allow to set overnight, then remove from the mold.

utensils

Large mixing bowl • Mold release • Large and small double boilers • Pouring can • Cold water bath • Weight and support • Wicking needle • Cork • Gas burner or blowtorch

ingredients

Pouring 1 16fl oz (500ml): 5¼ oz (160g) paraffin wax and 8½ oz (240g) stearin • Pouring 2 12¼ pts (7l): 11lb (5kg) paraffin wax, 17½ oz (500g) stearin, 1 orange fruit dye disk, 2tbs (30ml) mandarin essential oil, 1tsp (5ml) orange essential oil, and 2tsp (10ml) lemon essential oil • 20" (50cm) of 2½" (6cm) wick

Opposite: *To create the soapy surface effect, add far more stearin to the wax blend than normally recommended.*

62

one fresh orange

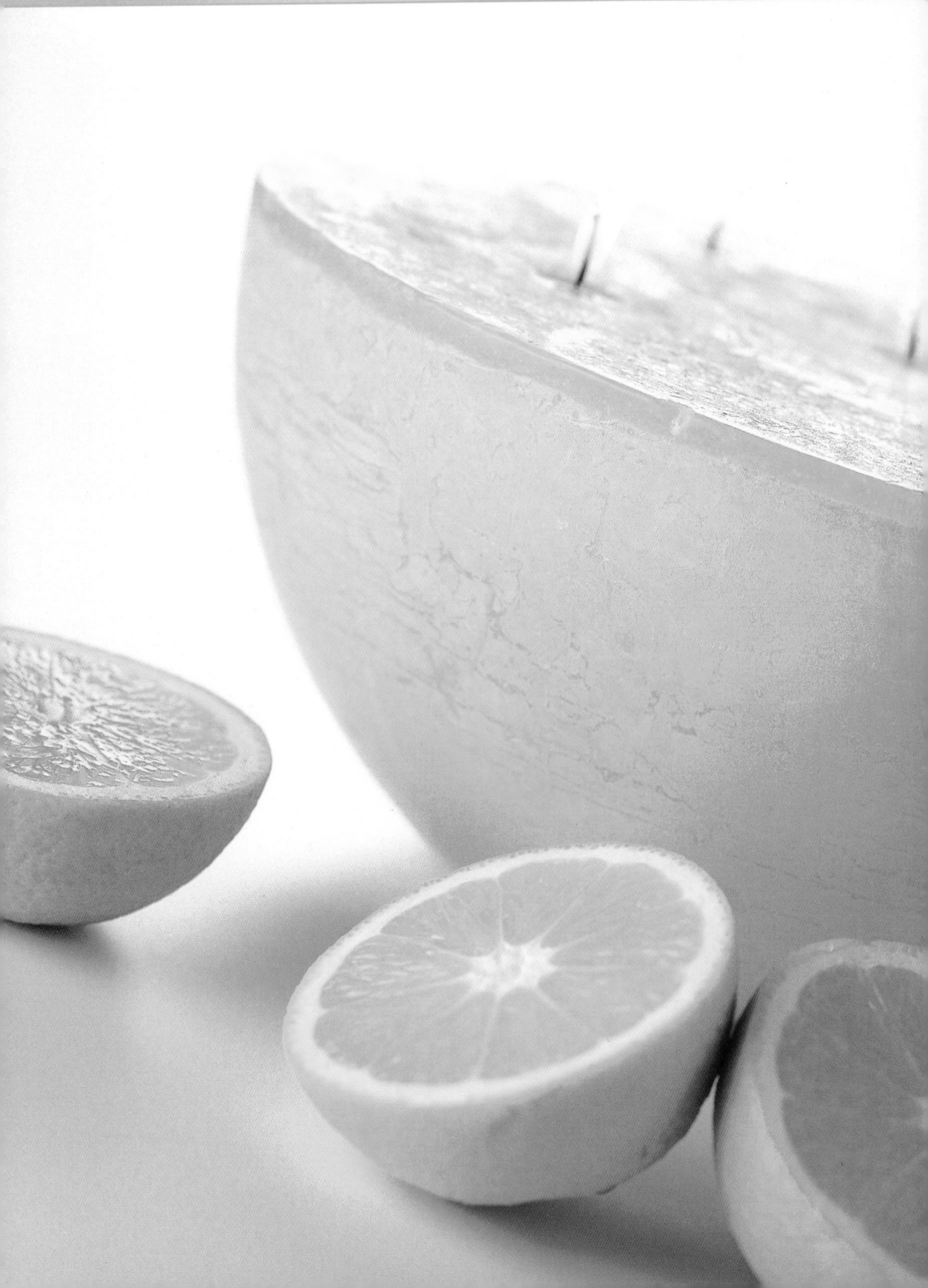

flava of jamaica

Sweet bay, deep red rum, and ginger provide the three Rastafarian colors red, gold, and green for the perfect Jamaican ambience.

one Make ¾" (2cm) ginger and rum chunks (see p. 68), dicing a couple of the ginger ones half that size—melt the beeswax to 154°F (68°C). **two** Draw around the inner circumference of the wide portion of the pipe onto the plastic lid. Cut this out and then cut a tiny square at the center point. Stick mold seal around the ledge where the pipe narrows and press the plastic circle onto it. **three** Coat the pipe with mold release and push the wick of the core candle through the hole in the plastic circle. Apply mold seal. Push the wicking needle into the base of the candle next to the wick, then secure it to hold the candle upright (see pp. 30–1). **four** Sprinkle small ginger chunks in the bottom of the mold. Pour molten wax down the side of the core candle to a depth of 1½" (4cm). Allow a thick skin to form. Press a layer of ginger chunks against the side of the mold with a knife. Submerge in wax by ¼" (5mm) and allow a skin to form. Add rum chunks and submerge by 1½" (4cm), then repeat with more rum chunks and submerge by ¼" (5mm). Insert a final layer of ginger chunks and submerge the core candle. Place in the warm water bath for 24 hours, weighting it down. **five** Remove the candle from the mold. Stand it on the food can and set the heat gun to its lowest temperature. Wave the hot air over the central bare band and press bay leaves into the molten wax. Play the hot air over the rest of the candle to produce the drips. Planish the base (see p. 27) and cure for at least 24 hours.

utensils

Double boiler • Rectangular mold • Chopping board • Large kitchen knife • 4" (10cm) plumber's soil pipe extension • Plastic lid • Fine marker pen • Strong scissors • Mold seal • Mold release • Wicking needle • String • Masking tape • Deep warm water bath • Weight • Heat gun or blowtorch • Food can narrower than mold • Old iron or frying pan

ingredients

Ginger chunks: 8½oz (250g) jelly wax, 2tsp (10ml) orange jelly wax, 2tsp (10ml) yellow jelly wax, and ½ tsp (2.5ml) red jelly wax • Rum chunks: 8½oz (250g) jelly wax, 2tsp (10ml) orange jelly wax, 4tsp (20ml) red jelly wax, and 1½ tsp (7.5ml) green jelly wax • Candles: 2¼lb (1kg) beeswax and 2 x 9" (5 x 23cm) core candle • Pressed bay leaves

Opposite: *Combining jelly wax with solid wax creates a stained-glass effect when the candle is lit. But the candle will fall apart if there is too much jelly wax.*

orange and lemon slices

An orange and lemon jelly wax mosaic sets off dried slices
of real orange and lemon, flavored with lemon and mandarin.
Made using the same utensils, and a similar method to Flava of
Jamaica on p. 64, this crisp white candle is a sorbet in the sun.

ingredients

*35½oz (1kg) paraffin wax • 3½oz
(100g) stearin • ¹⁄₃₂ oz (1g) chalky
white dye powder • Core candle, 2 x 9"
(5 x 23cm) approx • 8¼oz (250g) jelly
wax • Small dried orange slices • Small
dried lemon slices • 1 tsp (5ml) orange
jelly wax • 1 tsp (5ml) yellow jelly wax
• 1 tsp (5ml) essential oil of mandarin •
1 tsp (5ml) essential oil of lemon*

one Set up the mold and core candle as for the Flava
of Jamaica overleaf, omitting mold release. Prepare ½"
(1cm) chunks of yellow and orange-flavored jelly wax
as described on p. 68; divide the 9oz (250g) plain wax
into two and add the colors separately to each half.
two Melt 32oz (900g) wax and the stearin and dye, to
around 154°F (68°C). Melt the remaining 3½oz
(100g) plain paraffin wax to around 158°F (70°C) in a
separate shallow container. Switch off heat under the
white wax blend, and add the essential oils. Stir well,
and pour wax into the mold to a depth of around ¾"
(2cm). **three** Wait for a thick skin to form, then drop
in a sparse ring of yellow wax chunks. Dip three to
seven orange slices into plain molten wax one by one
and use a long knife to press each one firmly against
the side of the mold to form an evenly spaced ring.
four Add more wax and chunk layers until the slices
are submerged, and then add one more layer of
chunks. Leave gaps between the jelly wax to
strengthen the candle. Wait for a strong skin to form,
and pour in a ¾–1½" (2–4cm) layer of wax, depending on the depth required for the second layer. Allow
a thick skin to form. **five** Repeat steps three and four
with the orange chunks and lemon slices. Refill with
white wax to the base of the core candle, leave
overnight, and finish as before.

lemon grass

Tinged with a fresh spring green, this delicate column of vanilla-colored wax is scented with lemon grass essential oil, and iced with lightly tinted chunks of jelly wax. The method and utensils are similar to those of the Flava of Jamaica candle on p. 64.

ingredients

30oz (850g) paraffin wax • 1¾oz (50g) beeswax • 3½oz (100g) stearin • Core candle, 2 x 9" (5 x 23cm) approx • 9oz (250g) plain jelly wax • A little yellow jelly wax • ¼ tsp (5ml) green jelly wax • 1 pack freeze-dried lemon grass • 2tsp (10ml) essential oil of lemon grass

one Set up the mold and core candle as before, omitting mold release. Prepare ¾" (2cm) chunks of jelly wax as described on p. 68, adding around ¼tsp (1.25ml) green jelly wax and a little blob of yellow to achieve a translucent pale lime-green shade. two Melt the paraffin wax, beeswax, and stearin to around 154°F (68°C). While waiting for the wax blend to melt, peel off outer layers of lemon grass to reveal undamaged leaves, and trim off the tops. When the wax has melted, switch off heat, and add essential oils. Check the depth to which the tops of the stems will come inside the mold, stir the wax blend well, then pour to just above this depth. three Wait for a thick skin to form, and then dip the lemon grass stems into the molten wax one by one, pressing against the side of the mold and holding in position until the wax sets. Position so that the bulb of each stem is around ½" (1cm) lower than the base of the core candle, with the leafy top gently pressed into the wax skin below. Space 1¼" (3cm) apart. four Place one jelly wax chunk in each gap between stems, and pour in wax to submerge the chunks by around ¼" (5mm). five Wait for the skin to form each time, and keep repeating step four until the final chunk layer lies just below the bulbs of the lemon grass stems. Refill with wax to the base of the core candle, leave overnight, and finish as before.

jelly feast

Fun and fabulous, this feast of strawberry and orange-colored jelly wax would make a great centerpiece for a summer party— but be sure to keep it out of children's reach because the chunks of wax look delicious enough to eat.

utensils

Double boiler • Rectangular mold • Chopping board • Large kitchen knife • Pliers • Epoxy resin glue • Wicking needle • 2¼ lb (1kg) capacity square glass vase

ingredients

Strawberry chunks: 17½ oz (500g) jelly wax, 4fl oz (100ml) red jelly wax, and 2tsp (10ml) yellow jelly wax • Orange jelly: 17½ oz (500g) jelly wax, 4tsp (20ml) orange jelly wax, 2tsp (10ml) yellow jelly wax, and 1tsp (5ml) red jelly wax • Finely ground sea salt • Large container candle wick and sustainer

Opposite: There is no limit to the number of colors you could combine using this technique. Sadly, though, due to the high melting temperature of the wax, you can't add candle perfume.

one Make the strawberry chunks by melting the plain jelly wax in a double boiler and adding the colors. Stabilize the temperature at 203°F (95°C), then pour into the rectangular mold. Allow to set for two hours, then remove from the mold and chop into large chunks by placing the knife right across the block and pressing down firmly. **two** Put some salt into the mold and roll the chunks in it to simulate a sugar coating. Salt makes fire burn a degree or two hotter than usual, so shake off excess. **three** Melt the orange wax blend while you prepare the wick and sustainer, gluing them to the base of the vase and supporting the wick upright (see pp. 36–7). Cut the strawberry chunks in half and arrange two layers around the bottom of the vase with their unsalted faces pointing outward. When the orange wax reaches 203°F (95°C), pour it carefully down the wick into the vase. Fill to halfway up the second layer of chunks, then allow to set a little. **four** Arrange two more layers of cut strawberry chunks around the outside of the vase, then pour in more orange wax, repeating until the candle is about 1" (2.5cm) from the top of the container. **five** When set solid but slightly warm, pour in enough orange to cover the surface of the candle and arrange the remaining chunks on top. Flow in another thin layer of orange jelly to glue their bases firmly in place.

fizzy vine

Perfect for a summer party, brew up a big batch of fizzy vine. Bubbling over with intoxicating grape juice and cinnamon flavors, it's alcohol-free, and chilled ...

utensils

Tall square mold • Wicking needle • Mold seal • Double boiler • Cold water bath • Weight • Dipping can • Water bath • Kettle

ingredients

For every 7oz (200g) paraffin wax: 1/16th black grape dye disc, 3/4 oz (20g) stearin, 20 drops grape candle perfume, 10 drops cinnamon candle perfume • Overdip: 7oz (200g) stearin • Wick to suit

one Set the wax blend—minus the perfumes—to melt, and prime the wick. Prepare the mold as described in pp. 30–1, with around 2" (5cm) excess wick at the bottom of the mold. **two** Stabilize the temperature of the wax at 155–158°F (68–70°C), add the perfumes, and pour the candle quickly. Place in the water bath, weight down and leave to cool, topping up as necessary. Clean the double boiler thoroughly, ready for the next stage. **three** Once the candle has completely set (this should take roughly two hours), remove from the mold and heat-planish the base as described on p. 27. Set the stearin overdip to melt in your double boiler and boil the kettle. **four** Place the dipping can in its hot water bath, and fill with hot water to a level where the candle can be completely submerged. Once the stearin has melted, carefully float this on top of the hot water. Stabilize temperature at 180°F (82°C), then smoothly dip the candle right through the stearin pool and out again in one movement. Wait for thirty seconds and repeat. **five** Smooth away any drips from around the base of the candle while still warm. Once the overdip has crystallized, trim the wick and the candle is ready to use.

Opposite: *Fizzy vine's frothy finish is achieved in two stages: first, the body of the candle is poured as cool as possible to make a rough texture. Then it is overdipped in plain stearin, to create a crystalline layer of bubbles.*

café crème

A simple inclusion candle can be easily made in a mold using coffee beans or any small seeds, grains, or pebbles. Coffee beans make an ideal candle inclusion for leisurely dining—just be sure to serve a quality coffee at the end of the meal as a fitting salve to your guests' heightened caffeine anticipation.

utensils

Double boiler • 4" (10cm) plumber's soil pipe extension • Plastic lid • Fine marker pen • Strong scissors • Mold seal • Mold release • Wicking needle • String • Masking tape • Deep cold water bath • Weight • Old iron or frying pan

ingredients

2¼ lb (1kg) paraffin wax • 1¾ oz (50g) beeswax • 3½ oz (100g) stearin • 2 x 9" (5 x 23cm) core candle • 8¾ oz (250g) whole coffee beans

one Set the wax blend to melt. While waiting, prepare the mold from the pipe and plastic lid, coat with mold release, insert the wick of the core candle, and support the candle upright. two When the wax reaches 180°F (82°C), pour it into the mold until it is two-thirds full. Allow it to set until a thick, leathery skin forms on top of the wax, then put in a layer of coffee beans about 1" (2.5cm) deep. Increase the wax temperature to 185°F (85°C), then pour wax around the beans. Add another layer of beans and refill with wax, repeating until the top of the core candle is reached. There is no need to wait for the wax to set between layers—adding the beans and wax in stages simply ensures that the wax penetrates each layer. three Place the mold in the cold water bath, weight down, and allow it to set solid. When using a core candle, it is rare that a candle should need refilling, but check in case too deep a well should form around the core and refill if it does (see pp.30–1). When the candle has set (this should take 2–3 hours) remove it from the mold and planish the base (see p. 27).

Opposite: *Coffee bean inclusions don't just look fabulous, they smell great, too. The flame of the burning candle gives off just enough heat to release the fragrant oils, filling the room with that wonderful freshly-ground aroma.*

sunflower seeds

For sensational black-and-white splashes in pure white wax, use unshelled sunflower seeds. Mix the masculine fragrances of eucalyptus and sandalwood for a cool Art Deco feel. Method and utensils are as for the café crème on p. 72.

ingredients

9 x 2¾" (23 x 7cm) Art Deco-style tapered column mold • 8" (20cm) core candle • 5½oz (150g) shell-on sunflower seeds • 17½oz (500g) paraffin wax • 1¾oz (50g) stearin • ⅟₃₂oz (1g) chalky white dye powder • 5 drops eucalyptus candle perfume • 8 drops sandalwood candle perfume

Coat the mold with mold release and insert the wick as instructed for the coffee candle on p. 72. Similarly, prepare the wax in the same way, this time adding perfumes just before pouring the wax into the mold. Fill to around three-quarters the length of the core candle, then wait until a thick, leathery skin has formed. Increase the temperature to 185°F (85°C) and add the sunflower seeds in 1" (2.5cm) layers in the same way as for the coffee candle until you reach the end of the core, then follow the same instructions for finishing the candle.

scent of the tropics

The tropical colors of gerbera blooms are matched by the heady scents of heliotrope, gardenia, and musk in this frosted pyramid of flowers. The utensils are as for café crème on p. 72, but here the wax is stirred and poured cool for an icy surface effect.

ingredients

9 x 2½" (23 x 6cm) pyramid mold • 8" (20cm) core candle • Large handful dried baby gerbera • 14oz (400g) paraffin wax • 1½oz (40g) stearin • 5 drops heliotrope candle perfume • 5 drops gardenia candle perfume • 3 drops musk

Follow the coffee candle's instructions on p. 72, as outlined above. This time, however, allow the wax temperature to drop to 149°F (65°C) or so. Keep stirring until it begins to grow opaque, add the perfumes, stir rapidly, then pour the wax slowly into the mold to about two-thirds the depth of the core candle. When a thick skin has formed over its surface, position the gerbera flowers around the margin, pushing each one gently onto the skin to hold it in position. Refill with wax, then repeat until the wax is level with the core candle. It is important to arrange the flowers rather than simply pack them into the mold, or their petals will cause the inclusion layer to look dark and murky in a way that solid inclusions do not. Finish the candle as described on p. 72.

75

raspberry ripple

Deep folds of color in a marbled scoop, inspired by gorgeous dairy ice cream, make this candle an eye-catching centerpiece for a summer party. When lit, the fruit and vanilla scents are guaranteed to make everyone's mouth water.

utensils

2lb (900g) disposable plastic pudding basin • Mold release • Double boiler • Small pouring pitcher • Chopping board • Large kitchen knife • Cold water bath • Weight • Old iron or frying pan • Sponge scourer • Wicking needle • Cork • Gas burner or blowtorch

ingredients

Chunks: 12oz (350g) paraffin wax, 1¼oz (35g) stearin, 1¼oz (35g) beeswax, and ⅟₁₆ fuchsia dye disk • 20" (50cm) of 1½" (4cm) wick • Candle body: 17½oz (500g) paraffin wax, 1oz (25g) beeswax, 1¾oz (50g) stearin, 3 drops pineapple candle perfume, 5 drops strawberry candle perfume, and 5 drops vanilla candle perfume

one Coat the basin with mold release. Melt the wax blend for the chunks and add the color (see pp. 42–3). When it reaches 180°F (82°C), pour it into the basin. When solid but still warm, remove it from the mold, wash off the mold release, and pat dry. Chop it into uneven pieces. **two** Set the candle wax blend to melt to 160°F (71°C), omitting the perfumes for now. Clean the basin and reapply mold release. Arrange a bed of chunks in the base of the bowl and around the sides. **three** Prime the wick (see p. 28), then adjust the wax temperature to 180°F (82°C). Add the perfumes, then pour the molten wax into the center of the bowl. **four** Place the mold in the water bath, weight, and leave until a well forms in the center. Refill and repeat as necessary (see pp. 30–1). Finally, return to the water bath and allow to set for 4–6 hours or overnight. **five** Remove the candle from the mold and planish the surface (see p. 27). Buff firmly with a scouring pad to give a silky finish. Mark the three points of a triangle on the top of the candle for the wick holes, insert the wicks with a heated needle, and trim. **six** Once the wax has set, use the flat of the knife blade to shave off any surplus wax, then do a final brisk buff with the scouring pad.

Opposite: *Planish the wide, flat top of your marbled candle with deliberate abandon to achieve the drizzly effect of half-melted ice cream.*

nutty nougat

Delight and deceive your senses with this scrumptious-looking vanilla- and strawberry-scented slab of nougat. The scrape marks along its length make it look as if it has been freshly cut from a giant confectioner's block.

utensils

2½ x 2½ x 6½" (6 x 6 x 16cm) square column mold • Mold seal • Gummed paper tape • Thumb tack • Double boiler • Small pouring pitcher • Cold water bath • Weight • Large kitchen knife

ingredients

Halved glacé or candied cherries • Chopped angelica • Flaked almonds • 7 x 1½" (18 x 4cm) core candle • 10½ oz (300g) paraffin wax • 1oz (30g) stearin • ¹⁄₃₂ oz (1g) chalky white powder dye • Shavings of fuchsia dye disk • Strawberry candle perfume • Vanilla candle perfume

one Insert the core candle's wick through the hole in the mold, then apply mold seal. Stick the gummed tape halfway across the top of the mold, then set the wax blend to melt, adding the white dye (see p. 43). **two** Push a thumb tack through the tape into the base of the core candle to hold it central. Lay the mold on its side, with the taped half at the bottom, and sprinkle in some dried cherries, angelica, and almonds. **three** When the white wax is at 180°F (82°C), add a few drops of the perfumes. Transfer half the wax to a pouring pitcher, then slowly fill the mold to the level of the tape. Angle the mold so that you can pour the wax in, lying it down as it fills. Return any excess wax to the boiler and add the fuchsia dye. **four** When the wax in the mold forms a tough skin, press a few more inclusion pieces to the sides. Allow to set, then turn the mold over and add more inclusions on the remaining side. **five** Pour in enough pink wax to hold the inclusions in place, then stand the mold up and refill with wax. Place in the water bath and weight down for 1–2 hours. **six** When set, remove the mold seal, thumb tack, and tape. Drop the candle out of the mold and planish the base (see p. 27). Draw the blade of the knife over the surface of the candle to make scrape marks along the length of the bar.

Opposite: *Real angelica, glacé cherries, and flaked almonds combine with mouth-watering fragrances of strawberry and vanilla to make this nougat candle irresistible. Keep out of the reach of children!*

natural textures

lavender cylinder

This sleek, white cylinder candle is the perfect combination of contemporary and classic styles. The dried stem lavender inclusions make this a headily fragrant treat, perfect for lighting while you relax in a warm bath after a stressful day.

utensils

Double boiler • 5 x 3" (13 x 8cm) cylinder mold • Sharp knife • Mold seal • Masking tape • Thumb tack • Cold water bath • Weight • Old iron or frying pan

ingredients

To fill a 21fl oz (600ml) capacity mold: 10½ oz (300g) paraffin wax, 1oz (30g) stearin, and ¹⁄₃₂oz (1g) chalky white dye powder • 20 stems dried lavender • 2½ x 4" (6 x 10cm) core candle

one Melt the paraffin wax. While waiting, select enough flower heads to space evenly around the mold, and cut these from their stems. Cut the stems down so that they are fractionally longer than two-thirds the height of the mold. **two** Stabilize the wax at 172°F (78°C) and dip each flower head into it. Shake off the excess, then press to the side of the mold at about the two-thirds mark. Dip and attach a stem below each one. Work quickly, and do not attempt to reposition—if they do not go in the right place first time, start afresh with another one. **three** Melt the stearin and dye and add to the wax (see pp. 42–3). Stabilize at 176°F (80°C). While the blend is heating, insert the core candle into the mold, threading the wick into the wick hole of the mold and sealing it. Stick tape across the top center of the mold, and push a thumb tack through to help support the core candle in a vertical position. **four** Pour in molten wax, place the mold in the cold water bath, weight down, and refill as required (see pp. 30–1). **five** Once the candle is set, remove it from the mold and trim the ends of the stems to ⅛ " (3mm) above the base with a sharp knife. Planish the base (see p. 27).

Opposite: *The lavender heads are encased in wax, and therefore moisture-proof, making this an ideal candle for the bathroom. In both making and using, you will be amazed by the strength of the scent released by these few blooms.*

cinnamon

The rich, spicy scent of enlivening cinnamon brings an aroma of home baking to intimate evenings. The utensils and method for this candle are exactly as for the lavender candle described on p. 82.

ingredients

To fill a 21fl oz (600ml) capacity mold: 10½oz (300g) paraffin wax, 1oz (30g) stearin, and ⅟₃₂oz (1g) chalky white dye powder • 30 cinnamon sticks • 2½ x 4" (6 x 10cm) core candle

one Prepare the wax blend and core candle in the same way as for the lavender candle on p. 82. **two** Stabilize the wax at 180°F (82°C) and pour it to a third of the mold's depth. **three** Allow it to form a tough skin, then arrange cinnamon sticks around the core candle, butting them up against each other while still leaving enough room between them for the wax to flow. **four** Heat the remainder of the molten wax to 185°F (85°C), pour in, and finish the candle in the same way as the lavender one.

rosemary

The delicate needles of rosemary have a sharp, invigorating scent. Dry fresh sprigs from the garden, and use them to bring summer's freshness to the night. Utensils and method are as for the lavender candle on p. 82.

ingredients

To fill a 21fl oz (600ml) capacity mold: 10½oz (300g) paraffin wax, 1oz (30g) stearin, ¹⁄₁₆ pearly white dye disk, shavings of blue dye disk, and tiny pinch of chalky white powder dye • 10–15 thick, branched rosemary sprigs • 2½ x 4" (6 x 10cm) core candle

one Select the rosemary sprigs early in the morning, just after the dew has dried, and preferably in spring. Tie the sprigs together and suspend upside down in a dark, warm place until dry. This can take anything from a week to a month. Alternately, dry the sprigs in an oven or microwave, though this will remove much of the plant's natural aromatic oil. **two** Make the candle in the same way as the lavender version on p. 82, but do not pre dip the rosemary. Instead, arrange the sprigs around the mold, pressing them well up against each other to form a hedge all around. The thicker the distribution of rosemary, the better the inclusions will show in the finished candle. **three** Insert the core candle, then draw the rosemary sprigs back up in the mold until their tops lie around a third of the way down. **four** Pour in the molten wax at 176°F (80°C) and finish in the same way as the lavender candle.

millefiori magic

Millefiori canes of soft modeling wax are simply sliced and mold-ed to make this stained-glass fantasy. The neutral-colored core candle enhances the colors, with a pale core producing a pastel effect, and a darker shade of core resulting in a deeper glow.

one Make your own modeling wax (see pp. 20–1) or use colored beeswax sheets. Place them in the water bath and allow them to soften for 5–10 minutes. Remove the green and blue sheets and blot dry on paper towels. Knead the green and blue sheets together. **two** Roll out a ¼" (5mm) diameter sausage of purple wax on the glass sheet. Roll an ⅛" (3mm) sheet of yellow, and wrap this around the purple sausage. Trim the joint with a sharp knife before pressing well to make a neat seal. Surround with a thin sheet of blue-green in the same way, then make six pink and six yellow sausages of ⅛" (3mm) diameter. Press these around the core, then wrap another blue-green sheet around it. Roll to compact them. Finish with a thin sheet of yellow. Once well compacted, the cane should measure ¾" (2cm) across. **three** Place the cane on the cutting board, and holding the knife steady, roll the cane beneath it to cut the slices off. Apply slices around the wick on the top of the core candle, then work out and downward. Hold each slice in your fingers for a few seconds so that it becomes pliable, then press it against the core candle. Try to stretch and press each piece to the same depth for an even tone. **four** When the candle is completely cold, cover one face of the candle with a smooth polythene sheet and burnish its surface gently with the back of the teaspoon. Repeat on the other faces.

utensils

Warm water bath • Paper towels • Glass sheet • Rolling pin • Chopping board • Sharp knife • Polythene sheet • Teaspoon

ingredients

Purple, blue, green, yellow, and pink modeling wax sheets • Core candle

Opposite: *The thickness of the slices you cut from the millefiori cane affect the final look of the candle. Cut paper-thin slices for a delicate glow, or marginally thicker ones for greater vibrancy.*

frosted treasure

Sweet and subtle, this scrumptious sculpture of ice is quick, easy, and exciting to create. When wax is poured into the crumpled pocket of foil filled with ice chunks, it molds itself around them to produce wonderful frosty effects that are unique every time.

one Mold the core candle (see pp. 30–1), retaining ¾–1oz (20–30g) of the wax. Set the ice layer blend to melt and add the retained wax. **two** Roll a tube of aluminum foil, pressing the seam flat to make a wax-tight seal. Roughly squeeze the tube shut at one end, and push this end into the flowerpot. Squash flat. Put the lined flowerpot in the bottom of the bucket. **three** Wrap the block of ice in the towel and smash it with a rolling pin until the chunks are roughly ½–1¼" (1–3cm) across. Put a 1" (2.5cm) layer of ice chunks in the bottom of the flowerpot, then invert the core candle over this layer. Dig the wick down to the bottom of the pot, then fill to the base of the candle with more ice. Do not pack it down hard. **four** Set the temperature of the wax blend at 210°F (99°C), then pour slowly over the ice chunks around the core candle. Take great care because the wax is very hot. As you pour, a flood of wax and melted ice will emerge from the bottom of the flowerpot into the bucket. This is meant to happen. **five** Allow it to set for an hour, then remove the flowerpot from the bucket. Remove the candle from the pot and peel off the foil layer. Trim any little bits of stuck-on foil with a knife, and level the base candle if necessary.

utensils

Double boiler • 2½ x 4" (6 x 10cm) cylinder candle mold • Wicking needle • Mold seal • Cold water bath • Weight • Aluminum foil • 3½pts (2l) plastic flowerpot • 1gal (4.5l) plastic bucket • Dish towel • Rolling pin • Large kitchen knife

ingredients

Core candle: 17½oz (500g) paraffin wax, 1¾oz (50g) stearin, shavings of fuchsia and blue dye disks • 6" (16cm) length of 2½" (6cm) wick • Ice layer: 17½oz (500g) paraffin wax and ¼oz (5g) plastic additive • 1½pts (1l) water, frozen

Opposite: *A little of the core candle's color in the ice inclusion layer creates a real sense of depth. The process for making this candle is dramatic, and you never know exactly how it will turn out.*

cottage garden

A single specimen fritillary and dainty forget-me-nots ornament a pure beeswax cone to create a true cottage-garden display. If you wish, you could wrap a braid of green raffia around the base of the candle for an extra decorative touch.

utensils

Conical mold • Double boiler • Mold release • Mold seal • Wicking needle • Warm water bath • Artist's brush • craft glue • Damp tissue • Strong scissors

ingredients

Beeswax • Wick • Pressed cottage flowers

one Form the beeswax candle using the conical mold (see pp. 30–1). For an interesting ridged finish, as shown here, make sure the mold is cold before adding the wax, and pour every drop of wax down the wick. Any splashes that touch the wall of the mold will show in the finished candle. If you would prefer a smooth, glossy surface, ensure that the walls of the mold are thoroughly warmed through before filling. **two** Arrange the design of the pressed flowers loosely on its surface, then put to one side. Paint undiluted craft glue onto the central stem and bloom of the specimen flower, and apply this to the surface of the candle. Hold it in place until it firmly sticks, then carefully apply glue to the more delicate leaves, and carefully smooth these onto the candle. Lightly smooth down with a damp tissue, and wipe off excess glue. **three** Arrange some forget-me-nots or other small flowers in an informal array around the foot of the specimen flower, applying glue and smoothing down as before. (Forget-me-nots look best if applied to the candle back to front.) Allow to dry, then check for any loose areas and apply more glue. Finally, trim protruding stems level with the base of the candle.

Opposite: *Substitute pressed grasses or mosses to change the look of this delicate candle. Fritillaries, cowslips and many other wild flowers are available to buy from seed, so why not devote a corner of your garden to creating a wildflower meadow?*

wrapped in rainbows

Wrap a candle in textile trims for an opulent or home-spun look. It is essential to observe wicking dimensions, both for safety and to create the perfect, colorful glow. When the candle core has burned down, place a tea light in the remaining column of wax.

utensils

Double boiler • 5 x 3" (13 x 8cm) cylinder mold • Mold seal • Masking tape • Thumb tack • Cold water bath • Old iron or frying pan • Artist's brush • Craft glue

ingredients

1½ x 4" (4 x 10cm) core candle • 10½oz (300g) paraffin wax • 1oz (30g) stearin • ½₂oz (1g) chalky white powder dye • Yarn, ribbons, or other trim

one Using a readymade core candle solves the problem of safety. In addition, the chalky white powder dye used in the melted wax mixture does not burn well, and provides an effective firewall between the flame and the yarn. Insert the core candle's wick through the wick hole of the mold and seal. Apply masking tape across the top of the mold and stick a thumb tack through the tape and into the base of the core candle to hold it upright. **two** Melt the paraffin wax and stearin/dye blend separately (see pp. 42–3), then blend together and stabilize at 180°F (82°C). **three** Fill the mold with wax, then place the mold in the cold water bath and refill as required (see pp. 30–1). Planish the base (see p. 27). **four** To attach the textile trim, secure one end with masking tape and paint undiluted craft glue onto the candle's surface, pressing the trim down firmly as you go around. Wrap closely or sparsely, depending on the effect you would like to achieve. Once you have finished wrapping, secure the loose end with masking tape, too. For feather trims, or others that may be easily damaged by the tape, use a little piece of scrap paper to protect the trim when securing the ends. Once the glue has dried, remove the tape and if necessary apply more glue to the loose ends.

Opposite: *For a homespun feel, use deeply textured wool. For a light touch use silky ribbons or, for a funky look, try beaded trims.*

appliqué flowers

Quick and easy ornamentation transforms a plain readymade candle into this delightful floral display. The petals of the flowers have been curled slightly to give a beautiful, three-dimensional relief effect to the design.

utensils

Steel ruler • Sharp knife • Smooth cutting board • Flower cutter

ingredients

Base candle • Red, orange, yellow, white, and green appliqué wax

one Applying appliqué wax is easier if the base candle and wax are both a little warm. Wash your hands carefully before starting work. **two** Using a ruler and sharp knife, cut a long, narrow strip from the green wax sheet. Apply this to the surface of the candle, twisting and turning to suit the design, and pressing down well with your fingertips. **three** Place the orange and red wax sheets on the board, and with a flower cutter, cut out one piece of each color for each flower. Position the orange pieces on top of the red ones, staggering the overlap of the two so that the petals of each color are visible. **four** Position the flowers randomly along the stalk, pressing the center of each down well. **five** Cut leaf shapes from the green wax sheet, and apply these along the stalk between the flowers. **six** Roll a little yellow appliqué wax into a ball, and press this into position in the center of each flower. Roll eight smaller balls of white wax and press these around the yellow centers. **seven** Once all the elements are attached to the candle, gently prize up the tips of the petals with the point of the knife and curl them slightly.

Opposite: *Readymade appliqué wax is easy to use; if you are careful you can cut out your design freehand. If you're not so confident with a knife, cut a template from smooth tracing paper, then use a ballpoint pen to etch the outlines onto the wax before cutting.*

occasions

helter skelter

Make these sensational spiral tapers to delight your guests. Stick a handful in a pot full of sand for a simple, contemporary arrangement, or add to flowers for a stunning naturalistic display.

one Melt the candle wax to 160°F (71°C) and fill the dipping can. Cut, prime, and dip the wicks until each candle has a ¼" (5mm) diameter (see pp. 28–9). Working a pair at a time, hang the candles on a hook and wait for 30–60 seconds until the wax is just stiff enough to hold its shape. Quickly wrap the central portion of one candle's length around the pen four or five times, then repeat with its pair. Plunge both into the cold water bath for a minute until the springs hold their shape. Repeat for all the candles, then hang and dry them. **two** Dip the candles two or three more times, making sure that you do not allow them to linger in the dipping can for more than a second or two, and wait for them to grow almost cold between dips. Trim the ports as necessary (see p. 29). When finished, plunge each pair into the water bath for a rapid cool and allow to harden. **three** Melt the overdip blend with the tomato dye only. Fill the dipping can with just-boiled water to within 2¾" (7cm) of the rim, then carefully pour in enough molten wax to make a ¾" (2cm) deep pool on top of the water. Stabilize the temperature at 160°F (71°C). **four** Dip each pair of candles a couple of times, waiting 30 seconds between dips. Add half the fuchsia dye, allow it to melt, dip once more, then add the remainder and dip again. Plunge the candles into cold water and allow to set.

utensils

Two double boilers • Tall dipping can and stockpot • Hanging hooks • Fat, round marker pen • Deep cold water bath • Strong scissors

ingredients

Candles: *paraffin wax to fill dipping can and double boiler reservoir, plus 10% stearin* • 2–3' (70–100cm) of ¾" (2cm) wick per pair • Overdip: 7oz (200g) paraffin wax, ¾oz (20g) stearin, ¹⁄₁₆ tomato fruit dye disk, and ¼ fuchsia dye disk

Opposite: *Stir in the fuschia dye if you want an even shade of cardinal red, as seen here, or let it meander through the molten wax to create an interesting streaked effect.*

delight on diwali

Celebrate the festival of light with this sweetly fragrant gold-banded cone. A base of crystalline camphor inclusions is topped with a mixture of crushed cardamom and colored wax balls. The addition of a little beeswax to the candle's body adds still more sweet fragrance, and a delicate touch of ivory color.

one Melt the wax blend to 169°F (76°C). While waiting, insert the core candle wick through the mold's wick hole and seal. Apply a strip of masking tape across the mold's base and stick a thumb tack into the bottom of the core candle to hold it upright. **two** Pour wax into the mold to a depth of about 4" (10cm), and allow to set until a thick skin forms on the surface. Wrap a handful of cardamom pods in the dish towel and pound with a rolling pin. Roll little balls of the three modeling waxes and add these to the pods. Put a loosely packed ½ " (1cm) layer of these inclusions into the mold, pour in wax, then add another ½ " (1cm) layer, and cover with wax again. Repeat once more so that the finished layer is 1½ " (4cm) thick. Wait for a thick skin to form. **three** Break or cut the camphor blocks to about ½ " (4cm) across. Cool the wax until it is barely liquid. Loosely stack camphor pieces around the outside edge of the mold, then flow in the wax. Place the mold in the water bath, weight down, and cool for two to six hours. **four** Remove the candle from the mold, trim any protruding pieces of camphor, and planish the base (see p. 27). **five** Apply gilding size around the base and between the two inclusion layers. Apply gold leaf and burnish with a tissue (see pp. 40–1).

utensils

Double boiler • 3½ x 8" (9 x 20cm) conical mold • Mold seal • Masking tape • Thumb tack • Cold water bath • Weight • Rolling pin • Dish towel • Large kitchen knife • Clean, soft tissue

ingredients

Candle blend: 17½oz (500g) paraffin wax, 1¾oz (50g) beeswax, and 1¾oz (50g) stearin • Core candle, standard dining size • Green cardamom pods • Pink, red, and orange modeling wax sheets (see pp. 20–1) • Two camphor blocks • Gilding size • Gold leaf

Opposite: *An alternative to gilding size is to mask off and then spray with a light drift of spray glue. Place the candle inside a cardboard carton to minimize drift. Once the glue has dried to a tacky finish, apply leaf, and then buff off firmly to give ragged edges to each band.*

hanukkah stars

Frankincense and myrrh are released as these container candles burn, warming the gum inclusions. Make one for each of the twelve tribes of Israel, and arrange along a windowsill to welcome guests.

utensils

12 8fl oz (260ml) squat drinking glasses • Paper • Pencil • Masking tape • Baking sheet • Selection of brushes • Double boiler • Pliers • Shallow container • Burnishing tool

ingredients

Copper glass painter's outliner • Gold glass paint • Size • Gold leaf • Inclusion layers: 14oz (400g) paraffin wax, 1½ oz (40g) microcrystalline soft wax, 1½ oz (40g) stearin, 2 parts shavings of yellow dye disk, 1 part shavings of red dye disk, 17½ oz (500g) frankincense grains, and 8¾ oz (250g) myrrh grains • Candles: 3½ lb (1.5kg) paraffin wax, 5½ oz (150g) stearin, 5½ oz (150g) microcrystalline soft wax, ½ yellow dye disk, and ⅛ red dye disk • 12 small wick sustainers • 12 small container candle wicks, each ½" (2cm) longer than height of the glass • Self-adhesive copper strip • Shellac

one Draw the Star of David design onto paper, cut out, and tape to the outside of a glass. Trace the design with copper outliner on the inside of the glass. Repeat on the outside. **two** Fill in with gold paint. When dry, place the glasses on a baking sheet in a cold oven and heat at 325°F (160°C/gas mark 3) for 30 minutes. Switch off and allow to cool slowly. **three** Gild the design on the inside of each glass (see pp. 40–1). **four** Melt the wax blend and dyes for the inclusion layers (see pp. 38–9). Prepare the sustainers and wicks (see pp. 36–7). Stabilize the wax at 160°F (71°C) and switch off the heat. Pour a tiny pool of wax into the bottom of each glass, position the wicks, and support them upright with tape. **five** Working one candle at a time, mix 1¾ oz (50g) frankincense, 1oz (25g) myrrh, and a little shredded gold leaf in a shallow container, then drizzle over enough hot wax to make a paste. Press a ¼" (5mm) layer all around the inside of the glass. **six** Heat the candle wax blend to 160°F (71°C) and fill each candle to fill the glasses to within ½" (1cm) of the rim. Refill as required (see pp. 36–7) and set overnight. **seven** Clean the outside of the glasses if necessary. Apply copper strip to the rims, rubbing well with a burnishing tool. Apply gold leaf to the bases as before and protect with shellac.

Opposite: *The lining is a mix of microcrystalline soft wax and gum inclusions.*

advent pillar

This simple Advent pillar combines traditional Christmas red with contemporary, industrial, punched numbers. You need to work quickly, and be careful to keep a steady hand.

utensils

Paper towels • Double boiler • Dipping can and stockpot • Set of engineer's number punches, clean of grease • Small hammer • Cold water bath • Burnishing tool

ingredients

2 x 12" (5 x 30cm) readymade church candle • Overdip: 3½ oz (100g) paraffin wax, ¼oz (10g) stearin, ⅟₁₆ fuchsia dye disk, and shavings of tomato fruit dye disk • Gold leaf

Opposite: *Turning the heat right up just before dipping means that the bottom of the dipping can is hotter than the top. This causes the overdip to thin towards the foot of the candle. Before starting work, wash your punches thoroughly to remove all trace of the murky oil used to protect against corrosion.*

one Prepare a thick pad of paper towels on which to lay the candle. Melt the overdip blend and add the colors (see pp. 42–3). Fill the dipping can with enough hot water to cover the candle, then pour in a pool of molten wax. Stabilize the overdip at 185°F (85°C) at the top of the can, then turn up the heat under the stockpot so that the lower depths become hotter. Hold the candle firmly by its wick, dip 2–4 times, waiting 30 seconds between dips (see pp. 28–9). **two** As soon as the surface of the wax is hard to the touch, switch off the heat, lay the candle on the paper pad, and pick up the number 1 punch. Hold it against the surface of the candle at the top, and give it a light, sharp tap with the hammer. Repeat, tapping a little harder. If the punch sticks to the wax, wait a second or two, then try again. Repeat with each number in turn, moving down the candle as rapidly as you can. **three** Plunge the candle into the cold water bath for 30 seconds, until the overdip is hard. Blot dry the bottom. By this time, the overdip should have cooled to 180°F (82°C). Dip just the base of the candle 2–3 times until a band of solid red is created. Dip briefly into the cold water, then lay the candle on the pad. **four** Use burnishing tool to apply a ¼" (5mm) rim of gold leaf around the border of the dipped band, then apply ½" (1cm) squares onto the band (see pp. 40–1).

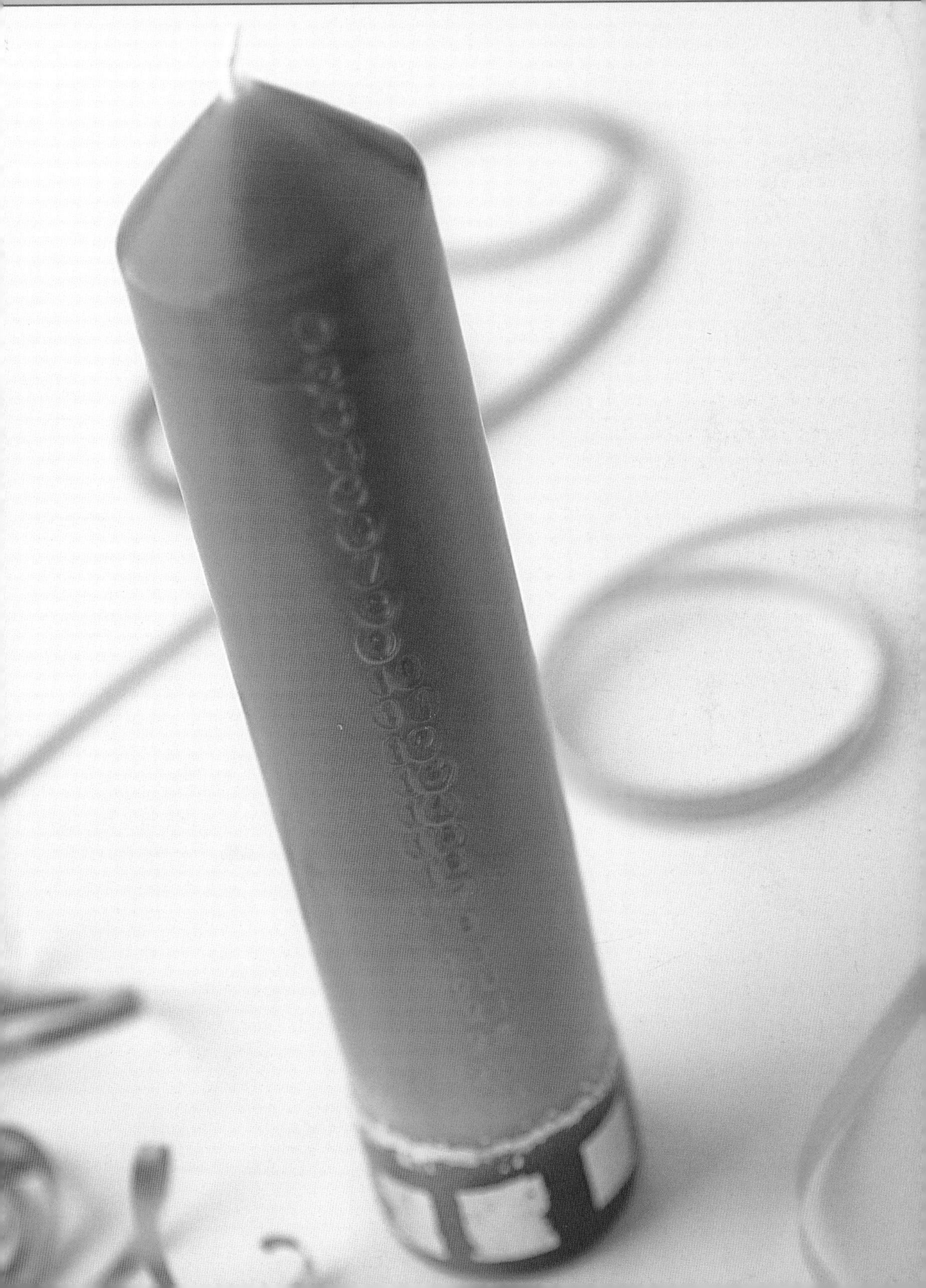

easter eggs

The miracle of Easter has powered Christianity for two millennia—and still inspires. Pay tribute to this ancient mystery with your own modern magic, of the engineering kind.

utensils

Teaspoon • Double boiler • Empty egg box • String • Masking tape • Sharp knife • All-purpose clear glue • Whole dye disk of any strong color

ingredients

Whole goose eggs • Per egg: 2⅔ oz (75g) paraffin wax, ⅓ oz (10g) microcrystall-ine soft wax, and shavings of pearly white dye disk • Small container candle wicks • Small wick sustainers • One box of size 10 lead fishing weights per egg

one Tap gently on the pointed tip of each egg with the back of a teaspoon and use the handle of the spoon to lever off small fragments, protecting neighboring areas with the pad of your thumb. Wash the shells thoroughly and peel away the inner membranes. Allow to dry. **two** Melt the waxes, prime the wicks, and attach the sustainers (see pp. 36–7). Pour the lead weights into the bottom of the shells so that they can stand upright. Pour a small pool of wax into the bottom to cover the weights. Put a sustainer centrally into each pool, holding the egg until the wax sets. Stand the eggs in the empty box with the weighted portion at the bottom. Support the wicks with tape and string (see pp. 36–7). **three** When the wax is 160°F (71°C) or cooler, spoon slowly into each egg. When you are ¾" (2cm) from the top, add the pearly white dye to the remaining wax (see pp. 42–3). Cover the top of the candle with wax, then refill any well that forms and allow to set (see pp. 36–7). Remove the wick supports and trim. **four** Rub the center of gravity at the bottom of the shell onto the dye disk to mark the spot exactly. Invert the egg and insert the point of a knife into the mark, twisting it gently to open a ¼–½" (5–10mm) hole. Squirt glue inside and hold it upside down until it sets. Turn the egg the right way, and stand it on the flat pad of glue.

Opposite: *The finished eggs stand level on tiny bases, made by pads of glue. The lead weights inside hold them upright.*

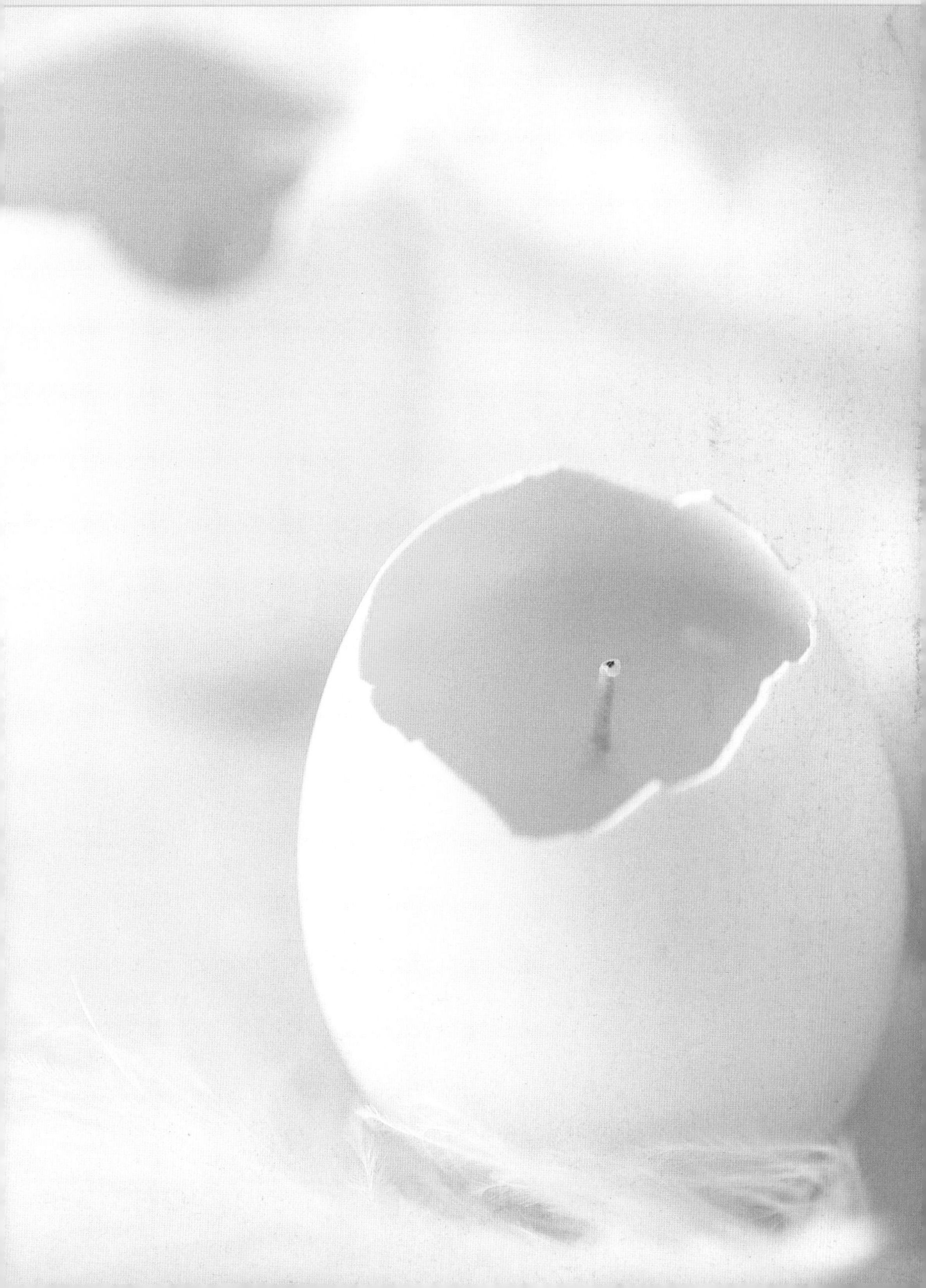

garden lights

rustic taper

Choose a glossy tree branch to act as the perfect foil for an untamed taper. A sculptural branched pole, like the one used in this project, provides twice the light. Try to get this season's wood because green wood is highly fire-resistant.

one Pick poles whose branches are ¾–1" (1.5–2.5cm) in diameter, and growing at a wide angle. Each one should be 12" (30cm) longer than the finished taper. Cut the base at a 45° angle, and saw the branches neatly square. Snip off loose fibers with garden clippers. **two** Wrap lengths of wet paper tape around the area you wish to coat with wax, pressing it down firmly and over the cut end. Allow to dry. **three** Melt the plain wax to 160°F (71°C) and fill the dipping can. Prime the wick and dip each taper until the diameter is 1" (2.5cm) greater than before (see pp. 28–9). Use masking tape to stick one end of the wick to the top of the taper, with 1¼" (3cm) protruding. Wrap the wick around the taper in 1" (2.5cm) coils, then secure at the bottom with tape. **four** Continue dipping until the taper is 2½" (6cm) thick, making sure that the top of the wick is clear of wax. **five** Melt the blend for the first pouring to 180°F (82°C) in a large can. Half fill a small can, and holding the pole upside down over the larger one, cover the taper with two or three coats (see pp. 34–5). **six** Melt the blend for the second pouring to 151–158°F (66–70°C) and repeat the pouring process, but this time dribble wax slowly over the taper without twisting it. Use a sharp knife to neaten the base of each taper. **seven** Cut a narrow scalloped border from appliqué wax, and press around the base of each taper.

utensils

Handsaw • Secateurs • Double boiler • Large dipping can and stockpot • Masking tape • Two large and two small cans with spouts • Sharp knife

ingredients

Branched coppiced poles • Plain paraffin wax to fill dipping can • Gummed paper tape • 20" (50cm) of 2" (5cm) wick per taper • Pouring 1: 7oz (200g) paraffin wax, 2 parts shavings of blue dye disk, and 1 part shavings of fuchsia dye disk • Pouring 2: 3½ oz (100g) paraffin wax, 3½ oz (100g) beeswax, and 8 parts shavings of blue dye disk • Blue appliqué wax sheet

Opposite: *Two variations on the basic pouring technique are used to decorate these dipped tapers. Pouring hot wax over a rotating candle gives even, thin coats. Dripping cool wax over a static candle makes for a dramatic stalagmite effect.*

glowing armada

Whether a modest half-barrel or the overgrown lake of a family estate, a flotilla of tiny, twinkling candles transforms any pond into a magical ocean—and your guests into giants on a Lilliputian shore.

one Wash and dry the pastry cutters. Tape the polythene sheet to a flat work surface and place the cutters on the sheet, blade side down. Press tiny sausages of mold seal around the outside face of the cutters' blades so that there are no areas where wax could leak out. **two** Melt the different colored waxes in separate cans, and pour into the cutters at 180°F (82°C) and to a depth of ½" (1cm). Allow to set hard but still warm. Carefully peel the polythene sheet away from the back of each one in turn, and throw the candles—cutter and all—into the cold water bath. **three** After 10 minutes, carefully press the shape out of the cutters and blot dry on paper towels. Neaten the shape with a sharp knife. **four** Insert lengths of wick using a hot needle (see p. 52), making sure that the wick enters the flat top at 90° and comes right through the candle. Try to make the hole as neat and narrow as possible. Hold the candles upside down and pour a little molten wax into the wick hole. Hold until the wax has set, carefully scrape away any stray drips from the top surface with a fingernail, and the candle is ready.

utensils

Pastry cutters in symmetrical designs • Masking tape • Polythene sheet • Mold seal • Small pouring cans and stockpot • Cold water bath • Paper towels • Sharp knife • Wicking needle • Cork • Gas burner or blowtorch

ingredients

½–1oz (15–30g) leftover colored wax per candle • 1¼" (3cm) floating candle wick per candle

Opposite: *Always use the special wax-coated wick for floating candles, and seal the base of the wick hole carefully with molten wax. Otherwise, water will enter the wick and extinguish the flame.*

tiny lights

For magic in the garden, hang tiny lights from old fruit trees. These sweet little lanterns are made from empty baby food jars, transformed with a little wire and a handful of beads.

utensils

Hot water bath • Clean, empty baby food jars • Double boiler • Pliers • String • Masking tape • Wicking needle • Strong scissors

ingredients

Each light: 3½ oz (100g) paraffin wax, ¼ oz (20g) microcrystalline soft wax, shavings of pearly white dye disk, and a few shavings of yellow, blue, or pink dye disk • Small container candle wicks • Small wick sustainers • Epoxy resin glue • Anodized craft wire • Copper wire • Two small pony beads or glass rings per light • Seed beads with holes large enough to accommodate two wires

one Warm the jars and make a candle in each (see pp. 36–7). **two** Make a double ring of anodized wire, just smaller than the bottom of each jar. Wrap wire twice around this to make a sturdy ring. **three** Cut a length of anodized wire to make a ring for the top of each jar. Thread on a pony bead, pass the wire through the bead twice more, then twist the two ends together to secure. Thread on some seed beads, then add another pony bead as before to sit on the opposite side of the jar. Thread on more seed beads, then twist the two ends of the wire together to form the correct circumference. Place the ring around the neck of the jar. **four** Cut 12 lengths of wire, each about three times the height of the jar, and bend in half. Twist these wires around the neck ring, with the seed beads divided between them. Take two neighboring wires and thread a seed bead onto them, then splay the wires to hold the bead in place. Continue in this way until you reach the bottom of the jar, then neaten the spacing of the wire-and-bead net. **five** Turn the jar over and slide the sturdy base ring over wires. Twist the wires around the base ring to secure, snipping off any excess. **six** Bend a length of copper wire into an elegant curve, loop the ends through the two pony beads, and squeeze shut with pliers to form the hanging handle.

Opposite: *Recycling was never so elegant. When pouring container candles into glass, it's essential to heat the jars first, and allow them to cool slowly.*

copper tapers

These modern-style cattail (bulrush) lights are created with copper and a fabulous verdigris effect. Make for the waterside, and reflect.

utensils

Gummed paper tape • Double boiler • Dipping can and stockpot • Masking tape • Three small cans with spouts • Sharp knife • Embossing mat • Embossing tool • Strong scissors • Pliers

ingredients

Craft-weight copper sheet • Butter • 5ft (1.5m) of ½" (1cm) copper pipe • Plain paraffin wax to fill dipping can • 12" (30cm) of 2" (5cm) wick per taper • Pouring 1: ¼ oz (10g) paraffin wax, ¹⁄₃₂ oz (1g) stearin, and 1 part shavings of black grape fruit dye disk • Pouring 2: 1oz (25g) stearin, 1oz (25g) paraffin wax, 3 parts shavings of blue dye disk, ³⁄₃₂ oz (3g) pearly white dye disk, 3 parts shavings of yellow dye disk, and tiny pinch chalky white powder dye • Pouring 3: 1¼ oz (50g) stearin • Epoxy resin glue • Heavyweight copper wire

one Rub one side of the copper sheet with butter, then lay it butter side up in the sun for a few days. Wrap paper tape around 4–6" (10–15cm) of the copper pipe (see p. 110). **two** Melt the plain wax to 160°F (71°C) and fill the dipping can. Prime the wick and dip the papered pipe until it measures 1¼–1½" (3–4cm) across (see pp. 28–9). Attach the wick as described on p. 110, with ¾" (2cm) protruding. Continue dipping until the taper is 2½" (6cm) thick, making sure that the top of the wick remains clear of wax. **three** Melt the first pouring to 172°F (78°C) in a small can and slosh it onto one or two points on the taper. Repeat to achieve a deep shade. Melt the second pouring 2 to 176°F (80°C) and pour over the taper (see pp. 34–5). Melt the third pouring to 176°F (80°C). Pour a few patches onto the taper, wait 30 seconds, then pour evenly over the whole candle as before. Neaten the base with a sharp knife. **four** Wash the buttered copper sheet, lay it on an embossing mat, and use an embossing tool to outline long, thin leaves on whichever side of the sheet you prefer. The leaves should protrude from a straight collar of copper measuring ½ x 6" (1.5 x 15cm). Cut out with scissors. **five** Apply epoxy resin glue to the copper collar, secure one end at the base of the taper with masking tape, then wrap tightly around. Secure the other end with tape and allow it to set. Trim protruding masking tape and bind the collar with copper wire. Tease out and arrange the leaves.

Opposite: *The stunning verdigris effect starts with a splash of black grape color. This is then overlaid with a greenish-turquoise, and topped off with plain stearin for the dusty look of corroded copper.*

angel's cup

This hurricane lamp uses deliberately blurred layers of colored wax to create a dreamy, sunset effect. Scented with sultry sandalwood and uplifting lavender, it's aroma is heavenly too.

utensils

Hacksaw • 4" (10cm) diameter plumber's soil pipe extension • 6" (15cm) length of 3½" (9cm) diameter plastic tube • Waterproof board • Mold seal • Double boiler • Two small pouring cans • Glass vessel • Cold water bath • Sharp knife • Pliers • Three 3½" (9cm) lengths of wire • Epoxy resin glue

ingredients

1lb (450g) paraffin wax • 1¾oz (50g) stearin • ¼oz (5g) microcrystalline hard wax • ½ tsp (2.5ml) sandalwood candle perfume • ½ tsp (2.5ml) lavender candle perfume • Shavings of fuchsia and blue dye disks • Tea light

one Saw a 6" (15cm) length from the wider portion of the pipe. Stick the plastic tube onto the waterproof board using mold seal around its inner circumference. Put the pipe, uncut edge downward, over the tube, and seal this around its outer edge. **two** Melt the wax blend (see pp. 18–19), then divide into the two pouring cans. Stabilize the temperature at 160°F (71°C), then blend the perfumes in the glass vessel and add a quarter to each can. **three** Pour 1¼" (3cm) of uncolored wax into the mold (the area between the inner plastic tube and the outer pipe) from one of the cans. Add fuchsia dye to the other can and pour a 1¼" (3cm) layer into the mold. **four** Divide the remaining perfume between the two cans. Pour a ½" (1cm) layer of uncolored wax into the mold. Add a shaving of blue dye to the fuchsia wax to create lilac, then pour a ¾" (2cm) layer. Add more blue dye to create sky blue and fill the mold. Immerse in the cold water bath until set. **five** Remove the outer pipe, then lift off the wax tube. Use a sharp knife to chamfer the top edge. **six** Bend the three wires into curves so that they can support the tea light's cup. Use epoxy resin to glue the wires to the base of the wax tube to act as a safe stand for the tea light.

Opposite: *The fragrant tube of wax shelters a tiny tea light from the breeze. You could also use a wax shell made like an ice bowl, using a mold constructed from two nesting pudding basins.*

angel's cup

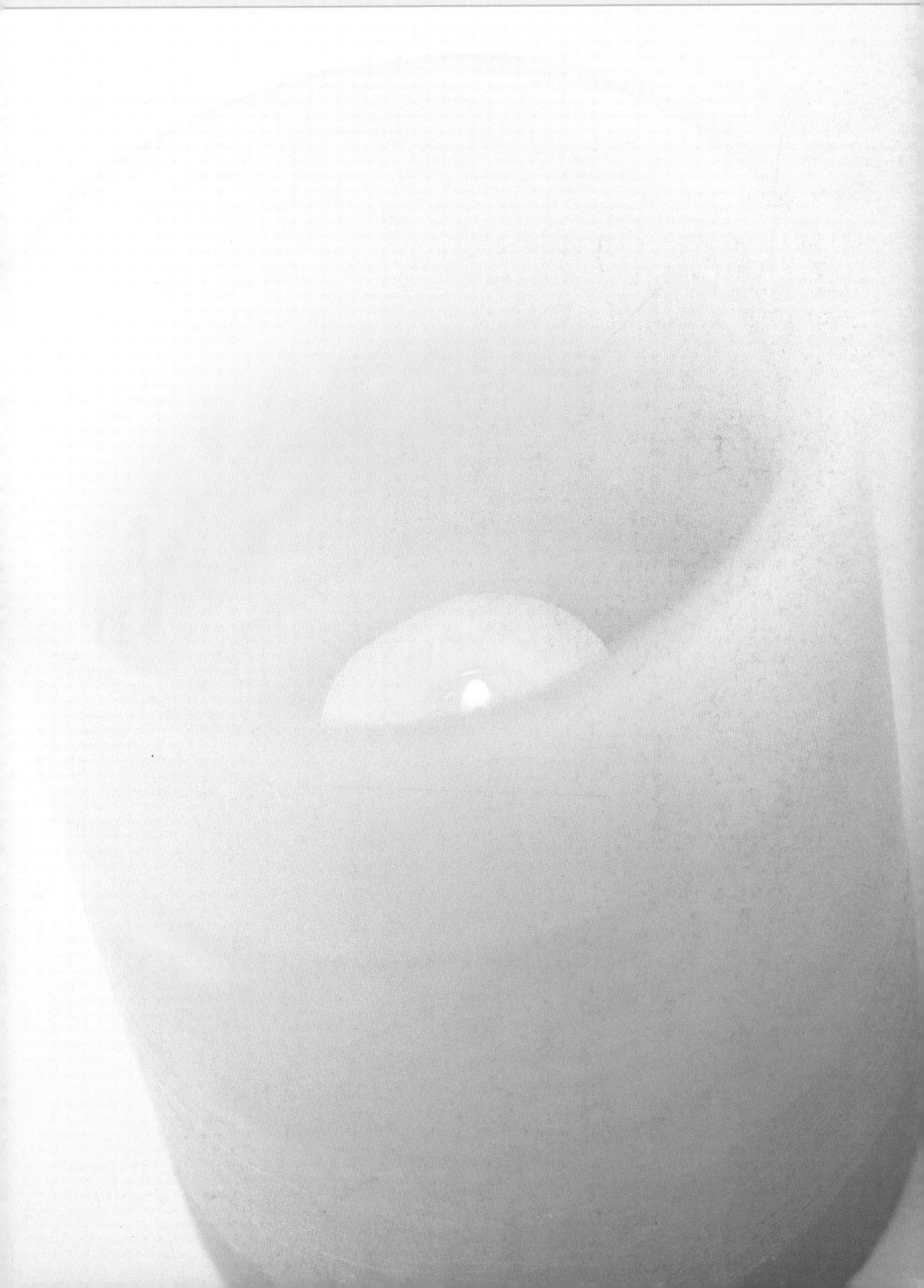

citronella flowerpot

A fly-repellent citronella flowerpot candle combines fire and fragrance to keep bugs at bay. These stunning floor-standing candles use a lot of wax and expensive essential oils, but you can easily scale down the quantities for smaller pots.

utensils

Large, clean terracotta flowerpot • Masking tape • Pliers • Strong scissors • Double boiler • Glass stirring rod or old spoon • Cardboard • Wicking needle

ingredients

Paraffin wax, plus for each 2¼lb (1kg) of wax: 3½oz (100g) microcrystalline soft wax, ½ yellow dye disk, shavings of green pepper fruit dye disk, 1tsp (5ml) citronella essential oil, and ½ tsp (2.5ml) lemon essential oil • Container candle wick • Wick sustainer(s) • Epoxy resin glue

one Seal the drainage hole inside the pot with masking tape. Calculate whether you will need to make a multiwicked candle if your pot is particularly large (see p. 20). Melt the first 2¼lb (1kg) of wax to 160°F (71°C), then prime the wick, attach a sustainer, glue into the base of the pot, and support the top of the wick in an upright position (see pp. 36–7). Adequate support is essential to prevent the long wick from sagging when the wax is poured in. When the glue has set, cut the wick 4" (10cm) longer than the top of the pot. **two** Add the colors and microcrystalline soft wax to the paraffin wax, then pour a little of the wax blend into the pot. Allow to set. Lower the temperature until the wax is barely liquid. Pour it into the pot, add the essential oils, and stir well. Cover the pot with cardboard. **three** When a well has formed in the middle, pierce the skin and refill with the next batch of wax (see pp. 30–1). Add the oils and stir, as before. Repeat until the candle is within ¾–2" (2–5cm) of its eventual level, and leave to set for two to six hours. When you refill this time, add the oils to the wax before you pour, and pour only as much as necessary to cover the previous layer. Allow it to set, then repeat once or twice more until there is no trace of a well. Remove all the tape and trim the wicks.

Opposite: *When making very large candles, whether in a mold or a container, add the wax little by little. Melting is then convenient on the stovetop, and the development of the central well is kept under control.*

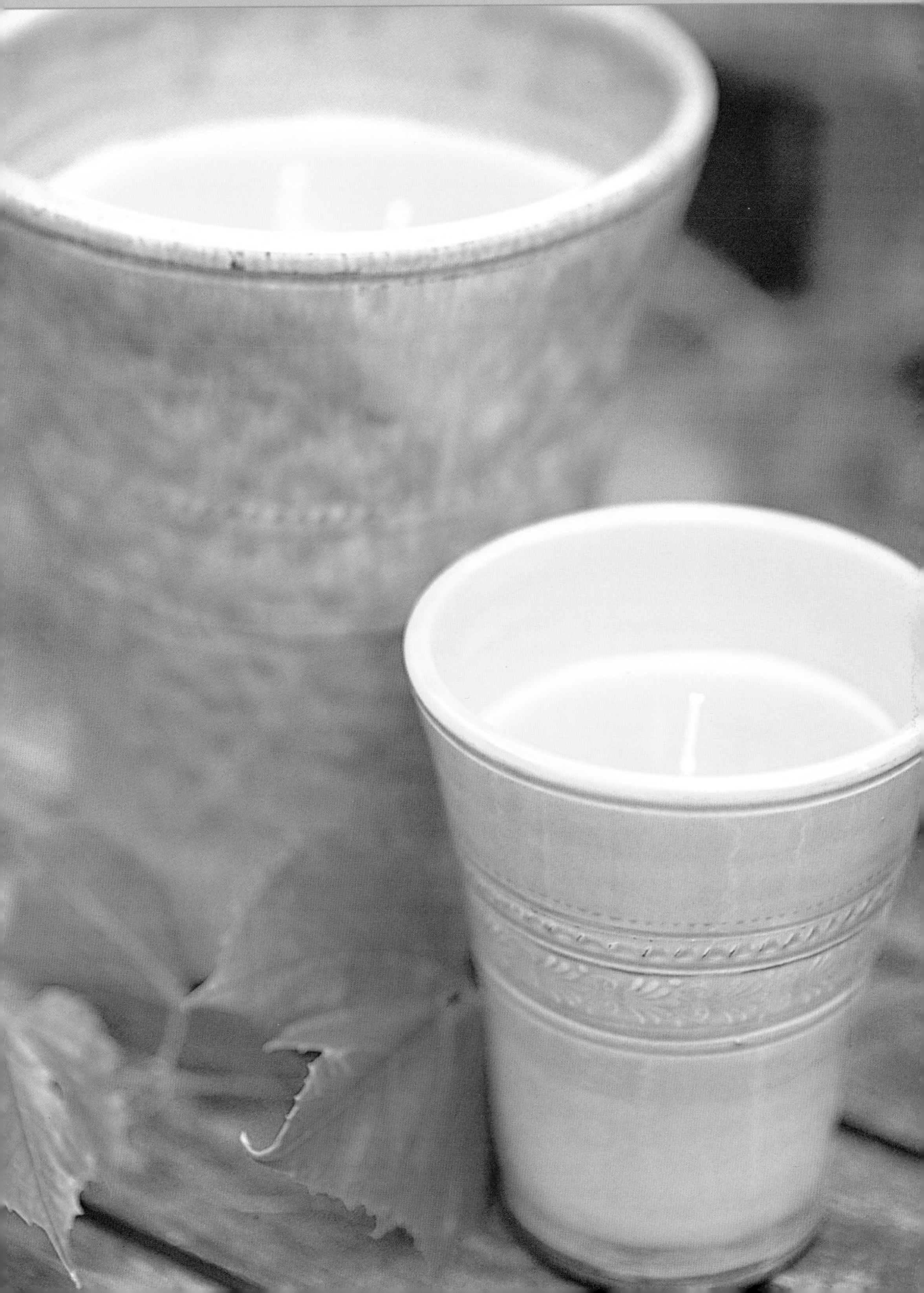

troubleshooting

When projects do not go according to plan, think of each difficulty as a steep step up the learning curve. There is a reason for everything, and as your experience grows, the problems will become few and far between. In the meantime, here is a rough guide to what might have gone wrong this time.

problem	explanation	solution
MOLDING		
Core candle wick will not go through mold's wick hole	Hole too small	Drill out or open with a bradawl
	Core candle wick too soft	Needs priming: dip into molten wax and draw straight with fingertips
White pitting on surface of candle	Water has entered mold	Start again
Candle stuck in rigid mold	Mold was overfilled on refill	Chill in refrigerator, then cut off overlaps
	Not enough stearin	Chill in refrigerator
	Paraffin wax: cooled too slowly	Chill in refrigerator
	Beeswax: cooled too fast	Start again
Candle stuck in flexible mold	Too cold	Place in hot water for a moment
	Needed mold release	
Cracks in candle	Paraffin wax: too cold when topped up	Start again and refill sooner
	Beeswax: cooling too fast	Start again with warmer bath
Layered candle poorly defined	Layers added too soon	Start again: wait for thick skin
Layered candle coming apart	Layers added too late	Start again: do not let it get too cool
Candle distorted	Air trapped in center	Start again: pierce and refill carefully
Surface looks like soap	Too much stearin	Enjoy the texture!
Surface scaly	Poured too cool	Enjoy the texture!

problem	explanation	solution
DIPPING		
Surface lumpy	Wax too cold	*Roll warm candle on flat surface, adjust temperature, and re-dip*
Wax slides down	Wax too hot	*Cool, roll, and re-dip*
Candle spits in use	Water in candle	*Pour off molten wax and re-light*
	Beeswax: propolis in wax	*Use cleaner wax next time*
MANIPULATING		
Candles crack	Too cold	*Re-dip or start again*
Candles will not hold shape	Too hot	*Wait a moment and try again, then plunge in cold bath*
COLORING		
Pink candle is too pale	Pink dyes only develop fully when wax is cold	*Wait and see*
CARVING		
Dipped layers separate	Candle too warm	*Stop and wait*
Wax cracks off surface	Candle too cold	*Work in warm room*
	Carving too deep	*Shave off tiny curls to build up design*

directory

US GENERAL EQUIPMENT AND MATERIALS:

Bitter Creek Candle Supply
Rt. 4 Box 184
Ashland
WI 54806
Tel: (715) 278 3900
www.candlesupply.com

Candles and More
Bobby's Craft Boutique Inc.
120 Hillside Avenue
Williston Park
NY 11596
Tel: (516) 877 2499
www.craftcave.com

Candles and Supplies
301 South 3rd Street
(Rt. 309)
Coopersburg
PA 18036
Tel: (610) 282 5522
www.candlesandsupplies.com

GB Mail Order
P.O. Box 2744
Orlando
FL 97402
Tel: (800) 456 7923
www.glorybee.com
(specializes in beeswax and beeswax equipment)

General Wax & Candle Co.
6863 Beck Avenue
North Hollywood
CA 91605
Tel: (800) 929 7867
Fax: (818) 764 3878

Hanna's Candle Co.
2700 South Armstrong Ave.
Fayettville
AR 72701
www.hannascandles.com

Missy's Candles
366 US Route 35
Ray
OH 45672
Tel: (888) 647 7971
www.candlemaking.com

Pourette Manufacturing
1418 NW 53rd Street
Seattle
WA 98107–3737
Tel: (800) 888 9425
Fax: (206) 789 3640
www.pourette.com

Rocky Mountain Candle Company
915 N. Lincoln Avenue
(Hwy. 287)
Loveland
CO 80537
Tel: (888) 695 5914

The Wax House
'Scent Masters'
15009 Held Circle
Cold Spring
MN 56320
Tel: (320) 363 0411
www.waxhouse.com

Yankee Candle Company
P.O. Box 110
South Deerfield
MA 01373
Tel: 1 800 243 1776
Fax: (413) 665 8321

US JELLY WAX SUPPLIES:

Kewl Candle Factory
1829 Kingshighway
St. Louis
MO 63110
www.gelcandlesupply.com
Tel: (314) 477 5258

CANADIAN GENERAL EQUIPMENT AND MATERIALS:

Ashburnham Crafting Supplies
120 Hunter Street East
Peterborough
Ontario K9H 1G6
Tel: (705) 742 6083
www.sympatico.ca

Lynden House International, Inc.
5527 137 Avenue
Edmonton
Alberta T5L 3L4
Tel: (780) 448 1994
Fax: (780) 448 0086
www.lyndenhouse.net

UK GENERAL EQUIPMENT AND MATERIALS:

Candle Makers' Supplies
28 Blythe Road
London W14 0HA
Tel: (020) 7602 4031

The Candles Shop
30 The Market
Covent Garden
London WC2E 8RE
Tel: (020) 7836 9815
www.candlesontheweb.co.uk

E.H. Thorne Ltd
Beehive Works
Wragby
Market Rasen
Lincoln LN8 5LA
Tel: (01673) 858 555
(specializes in beeswax and beeswax equipment)

Fred Aldous Limited
37 Lever Street
Northern Quarter
Manchester M1 1LW
Tel: (08707) 517 3000
www.fredaldous.co.uk

Hudnalls Apiaries
The Hudnalls
St. Briavels
Gloucestershire GL15 6RT
Tel: (01594) 530 807
(specializes in beeswax)

Stockbridge Beekeeping Supplies
Chilbolton Down Farm
Stockbridge
Hampshire SO20 6BU
Tel: (01264) 810 916
(specializes in beeswax and beeswax equipment)

UK WAX WHOLESALE:

Poth Hille
37 High Street
Stratford
London E15 2QD
Tel: (020) 8534 7091

UK NATURAL PIGMENTS:

The Green Shop
Bisley
Stroud
Gloucestershire GL6 7BX
Tel: (01452) 770 629

AUSTRALIAN GENERAL EQUIPMENT AND MATERIALS:

Southern Lights Candle Company
Boggabri
NSW 2382
Australia
Tel: (02) 6743 6518

AUSTRALIAN BEESWAX AND MOLDS:

Redpath's Beekeeping Supplies
193 Como Parade East
Parkdale
Victoria 3195
Tel: (03) 9587 5950

NEW ZEALAND GENERAL EQUIPMENT AND MATERIALS:

Golding Handicrafts
PO Box 9022
Wellington
Tel: (04) 801 5855

index